ZOMBIE WORMS AND BLUE DRAGONS

BLOOMSBURY CHILDREN'S BOOKS
Bloomsbury Publishing Plc
50 Bedford Square, London WC1B 3DP, UK

Bloomsbury Publishing Ireland Limited
29 Earlsfort Terrace, Dublin 2, D02 AY28, Ireland

First published in Great Britain in 2026 by Zephyr, an imprint of Bloomsbury Children's Books

A catalogue record for this book is available from the British Library

ISBN (HB): 9781035917235
ISBN (E): 9781035917259

2 4 6 8 10 9 7 5 3 1

Cover design: Gemma Gorton
Book design: Nicky Borowiec

Printed and bound in China by RR Donnelley, Dongguan City, Guangdong

MIX
Paper | Supporting responsible forestry
FSC® C144853

To find out more about our authors and books visit www.bloomsbury.com and sign up for our newsletters
For product safety related questions contact productsafety@bloomsbury.com

CELEBRATING 100 ICONIC SPECIES

ZOMBIE WORMS AND BLUE DRAGONS

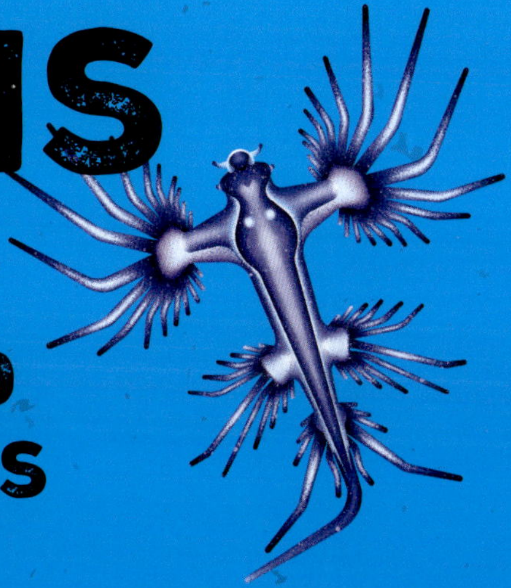

CELEBRATING 100 ICONIC LIFE FORMS

BEN GARROD EMILY HIGGS

ZEPHYR

For Seren, Lyra, Abi and all the other young women and girls
in science. We need you now, more than ever.

BG

As my first publication, I dedicate this to my incredible Mum &
Dad - Cathy & Ian - and my family, who have always encouraged my
creativity and championed my passion for the natural world.
Also, to my wonderful husband Jordan, who has been my rock
throughout this exciting illustrative journey.

EH

INTRODUCTION

Something important happened around three and a half billion (3,500,000,000) years ago. Scientists don't really know what, or exactly where, or even when this mysterious thing took place. But something started a process that resulted in the first life on Earth. In time, we'll discover more about this fantastic episode in the history of our planet and those first few moments of early life. We are far more certain about what happened next – once it started, life flourished.

From single-celled structures to complex, multicellular organisms, life expanded across the planet and before long inhabited every ecosystem imaginable: from the brightest coral reefs to the coldest polar regions, from the crushing depths of the ocean floor to the windswept ridges of our tallest mountain ranges. Life spread out and made its home wherever it found the space.

With so many different habitats, it was impossible for just one type of life form to succeed everywhere, so it did something truly incredible as it spread. It changed. It adapted, diversified and evolved to be better suited to countless habitats and the conditions in them.

It adapted to changing temperatures and pressures, to gases in the air and levels of salt in the water. Some life forms changed to live in the light and others to live in the dark. Some became able to withstand radiation from the sun: others found ways to live in poisonous environments. New life started affecting other life and before long, some life forms hunted others for food, forcing both either to change over time, or die out.

Some life forms harnessed the energy they found in others to evolve together. This ever-changing game of survival has, over the last three and a half billion (3,500,000,000) years, created an almost unimaginable diversity of organisms: living things, all at the mercy of the world around them, all connected, regardless of how small those links may sometimes appear. Our own species is just another form of life, no less and no more important than any other.

In *Zombie Worms and Blue Dragons*, I explore some of the differences we see across nature – something we call biodiversity. From the lightning-fast strike of the reef-dwelling mantis shrimp, to the bizarre courtship displays of the truly ancient-looking shoebill in its swamp, to one of the world's most successful organisms that's found flourishing in your home, nature is truly inspiring.

Ben Garrod (Professor)

NATURAL SELECTION

'Evolution' is a term you may have heard of and will probably have some idea of its meaning. Evolution is simply a *process of change*, in biology. That's it. It's not about *improving* a species, and it isn't *aiming* for anything. Evolution is what happens, over time, when a species or a group of species interacts with other species and their environment.

One of the best-known areas of evolution is something called *natural selection*. It's easy to think this is all there is to evolution, but natural selection is just one part of this vast and complicated natural force.

Throughout the life of every organism, every plant, animal, fungi and bacteria, tiny and random changes go on all the time. When our cells are copied again and again and again throughout our life, there will occasionally be errors or imperfections in the new copy. We call these 'mutations'. Often, mutations cause problems for an organism and they may not survive. Others are more neutral and don't really make much of a difference.

Some mutations are helpful and will do one of two things, sometimes both: they will help the organism survive and will improve its chances of reproducing and having young. For a bird, a 'good' mutation might be having a slightly longer beak or a curved beak, which helps it get more food. For an insect, it might be slightly larger wings or stronger muscles to help it fly faster. For a flower, it might be larger or brighter petals to attract more insects or birds to pollinate it.

Over time, a mutation that helps in this way becomes more and more common. If the mutation helps, there's a chance it will be selected, at a genetic level, in the organism's DNA. This might lead the mutation to become stronger and the adaptation becomes more noticeable or lasts longer, for example. Over time, the entire body or behaviour can be changed and eventually, this may lead to a new species. This new species may live alongside the older species, or in a new habitat. It might even take over and then the older species dies out.

Natural selection helps us understand how the Venus flytrap developed its trap to catch prey in places where the soil is low in nutrients. It also explains why the fiddler crab evolved one massive claw for display and how, over time, the mantis shrimp evolved to have a powerful punching club for stunning prey.

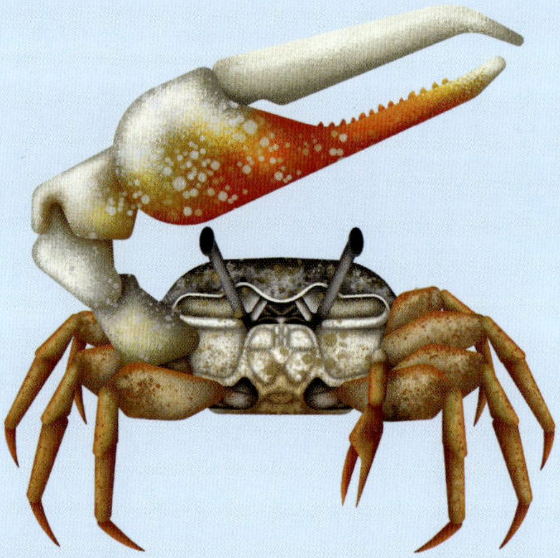

FIDDLER CRAB

VENUS FLYTRAP

MANTIS SHRIMP

CONVERGENT AND DIVERGENT EVOLUTION

GIGANTOPITHECUS

Evolution is the story of how and why life on Earth is the way it is but, like any good story separated into chapters, evolution is split into many smaller parts. An important area is the idea of convergent and divergent evolution. Understanding these two concepts reveals so much about why we sometimes see certain patterns in the life around us.

The word convergent (con-ver jent) means coming together. So, if you and your friends meet at a specific point, such as a bench in the park, and you've come from different places, then you are converging. Convergent evolution means coming together to look or behave in a similar way, despite coming from different starting points.

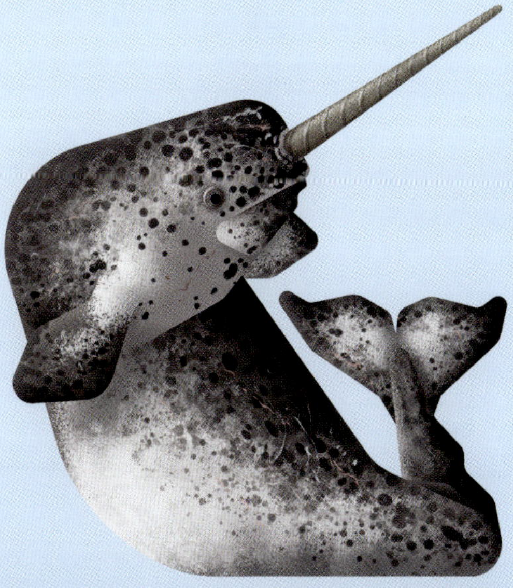

NARWHAL

If the habitat, environment or the influence of other organisms is the same for two species, it's possible those two species will show similar adaptations, even if they are thousands of kilometres away from one another or separated by millions of years. It also works if they are not closely related to one another. This impact caused by similar influences explains how completely unrelated groups appear to come together or converge in their evolution. Convergent evolution explains why two very different mammals, the *Smilodon* and the marsupial *Thylacosmilus*, both have large 'sabre-toothed' canine teeth, for hunting and display, despite being genetically separated from each other by over 100 million years. It also explains why insects such as the orchid mantis, birds such as the hoatzin, and prehistoric reptiles such as the *Quetzalcoatlus* all developed wings for powered flight. None of these are closely related *at all*, but each has evolved a way to fly using wings.

When we look at divergent (di-ver jent) evolution, it's the opposite to convergent evolution, almost. To diverge is to split up from a point, heading to different directions. In evolution, we see a split from what scientists call a common ancestor into different forms of either behaviour or anatomy. If we take mammals as a group, then it's clear we are all fairly closely related, so we have a known starting point. When we look at a limb, then we can see how the prehistoric mammal 'blueprint' has diverged, or split, over millions of years, creating hands in *Gigantopithecus*, hooves in the babirusa and flippers in the narwhal. These changes, from a single starting point, allow different types of mammals to diverge, behave differently and thrive in different habitats and ecosystems.

BABIRUSA

SYMBIOSIS (SIM BI-O SIS)

Nature is full of relationships that develop between different species and last over long periods of time. Not all involved in these relationships benefit from them. Symbiotic relationships come in three main forms.

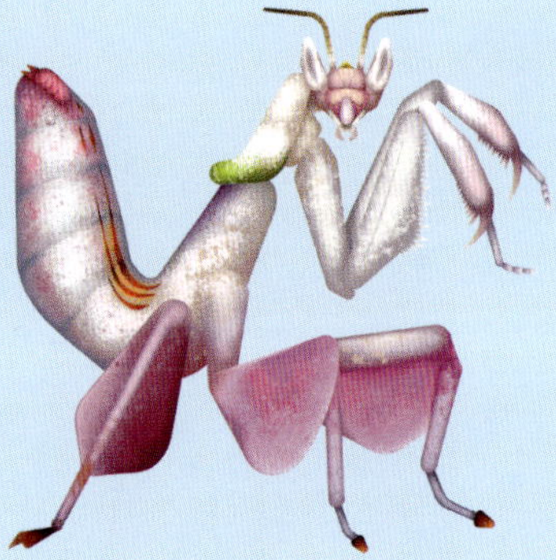

ORCHID MANTIS

MUTUAL RELATIONSHIP

In this form of symbiosis, *both* organisms involved in the relationship mutually benefit. It's a long-term, between-species cooperation. In this relationship, neither organism is harmed by being a part of the relationship. The ocean sunfish is a good example of mutualism. This giant ocean-dwelling fish picks up many different parasites, which feed on and live on its skin. Swimming to the surface and lying on its side, the sunfish will soon attract the attention of gulls and other seabirds. The birds pick off the various parasites. They get a meal and the sunfish has parasites removed, which would otherwise cause it many problems.

OCEAN SUNFISH

COMMENSAL RELATIONSHIP

In a commensal relationship, only one organism benefits. The other does not benefit but is not harmed. This can sometimes be a subtle or more 'gentle' form of symbiosis and it's not always obvious that there *is* a symbiotic relationship present. The orchid mantis is a good example of commensalism. It looks like an orchid and even sways like a flower in the breeze. It uses this mimicry to catch food and to avoid predators, and while the orchid itself does not benefit, it is not harmed.

PARASITIC RELATIONSHIP

A parasitic relationship is the most well-known form of symbiosis. It is, at its simplest, where one organism takes advantage of another, either through stealing from it, infecting it or eating parts of it. The greater frigate bird is an unusual type of parasite, stealing food from other birds rather than always hunting for its own fish. Clearly, the frigate bird benefits from this and the other bird suffers by losing a meal.

The reason we see so many examples of symbiosis is because nature is interconnected, like one giant web, with links and ties between species and groups of species. While it's clear that some symbiotic relationships are examples of one organism taking advantage of another, others allow all partners to benefit, increasing their chances of survival.

GREATER FRIGATE BIRD

COLONIAL ORGANISMS

FIRE CORAL

When we think of an animal, whether the smallest flea or the largest whale, we think of an individual. An organism is one living thing, feeding, moving and breeding as an individual.

Some animals, such as lions or penguins, live in groups. Others, such as some species of ant or bee, live in large, cooperative groups, called colonies. The ants work together, some look different and have different roles, but are still seen as individuals.

Then there are colonial organisms. These are made up of many, sometimes many millions, of smaller organisms working together as one. The difference is that although these organisms are still made up from individuals, the individuals cannot survive on their own. Many of the smaller organisms are completely different from one another and perform specific and different roles from one another. With many smaller, simpler individuals working together in this way, they form complex, larger organisms.

The fire coral is a good example of a colonial organism, where countless individual microscopic organisms create the tree-like coral structure. Likewise, being a colonial organism allows the Portuguese man o' war to be one of the most venomous organisms found throughout the oceans.

The smaller organisms making up a colonial organism are called zooids (zoo-ids), which are joined together and share nutrients. Some zooids move and can't feed, while others feed and can't move, but between them, they succeed in making a large 'super-organism'. It's the ultimate example of cooperation in nature.

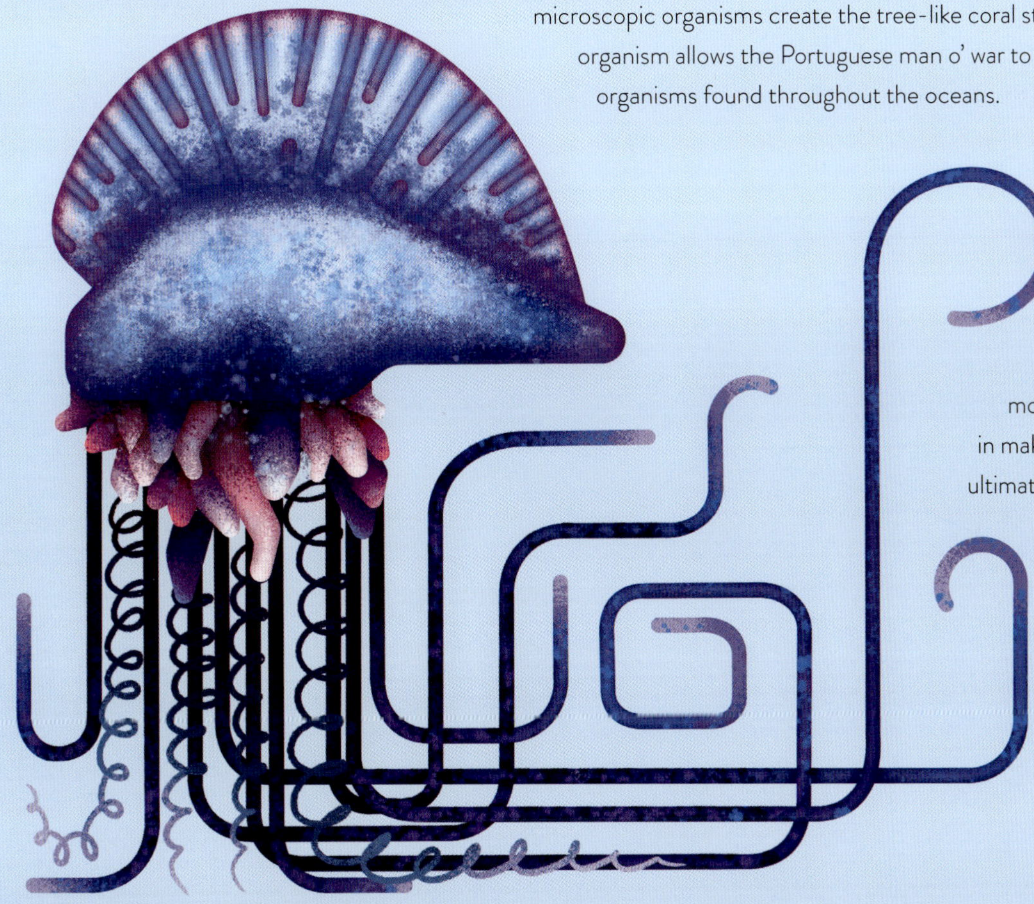

PORTUGUESE MAN O' WAR

MIMICRY AND CAMOUFLAGE

What's the best way to hide? Maybe blending in with your surroundings, so it's almost impossible to tell you and the environment apart? Or pretending to be something completely different, so that if something is looking for you, it wouldn't know it was you, even if it was staring straight at you? These two approaches are found throughout nature.

Camouflage is where you try to hide in a more classic way. You use bits of your surroundings, such as mud or leaves, to hide in, or maybe you adapt to be camouflaged, yourself. The potoo blends in so well with its surroundings that it is almost impossible for a predator to tell where a branch ends and where this camouflaged bird begins. Camouflage isn't just about hiding from predators – some predators use camouflage too. The tasselled wobbegong is an expert at blending in, and this flattened shark can wait for hours on the seabed until a fish swims by.

TASSELLED WOBBEGONG

When an animal uses mimicry, it doesn't try to blend in but instead looks like something completely different. Rather than saying, 'You can't see me', it's more a case of, 'Hey, I'm something else entirely.' Although it does also use camouflage, the cuttlefish is able to change its shape, looking like seaweed, a fish, or even a crab. It is able to change the colour and texture of its skin, making it a brilliant mimic.

The spider-tailed horned viper has what might be one of the most incredible examples of mimicry seen anywhere in the natural world, using a tail adapted to look like a tasty spider to tempt in a hungry bird. With a fat 'body' and spindly 'legs', this spider looks too good to miss, but when a bird gets close, they learn the hard way just how effective this snake is at mimicry.

SPIDER-TAILED HORNED VIPER

CUTTLEFISH

POTOO

YOU WILL FIND THESE SYMBOLS ON EVERY PAGE:

YA: Years ago

MYA: Million years ago

~: Approximately

☠ Extinct/Not alive

♥ Extant/Alive

🕒 Timeline

📍 Location

🍴 Diet

DIMETRODON

(Di-met ro-don)

EXTINCT
295–272 MYA
N AMERICA, EUROPE
CARNIVORE

Looking like a mix between a reptile and a dinosaur, this ferocious, ancient predator was actually more closely related to you and me.

Walking on four clawed legs and with a long powerful tail, *Dimetrodon* had a huge, rounded head, with many large teeth. The most striking part of its anatomy was a huge sail running along the back of its body. The sail was made up of long bony spines, one from each vertebra, connected by skin, and it could have been up to 1m tall.

There were a few different species of *Dimetrodon*, ranging in length from 1.5–4.6m. It could have weighed as much as 250kg, about the same as an alligator.

The teeth of *Dimetrodon* were different in different parts of the mouth and had different jobs. There were small, incisor-like teeth for gripping, big canines for stabbing and teeth at the back of its jaws for tearing and cutting meat. It also had teeth embedded into the roof of its mouth, which helped hold prey in place.

Dimetrodon was the top predator in its environment, and would have eaten fish, amphibians and reptiles.

The giant spiny sail may have helped warm or cool the body, although it was more likely used in dominance and threat displays and during courtship.

The last *Dimetrodon* died out around 40 million years before the first dinosaurs appeared on our planet.

SMILODON

(smy-l o-don)

EXTINCT
2.5 MYA–10,000 YA
N & S AMERICA
CARNIVORE

If you have a pet cat, you know cats are cute but they're not to be messed with. A tiger, the largest cat alive today, is even less likely to want a tummy tickle, but weighing almost twice as much as even the biggest tiger and having teeth like daggers might make *Smilodon* nature's ultimate feline.

At over 400kg, as much as a large crocodile, and 120cm tall, the *Smilodon* was a formidable predator. By looking at its fossilised bones, scientists think it used its massive teeth to kill its prey. Measuring 28cm, or nearly the length between an adult's wrist and elbow, these canines are the largest found in any cat. The skeleton of a *Smilodon* shows us it could perform ambush kills, leaping onto prey and using its long canines to stab into the neck or throat for the fatal blow. There are no preserved skins, but *Smilodon*'s coat is usually shown as being plain or spotted.

Smilodon was found across North and South America, where it hunted different prey. In the north, it hunted camels and bison, but may have had different prey in the south, including giant ground sloths. It's unlikely the large canines caused problems when eating, as many cat species eat their food through the side of the mouth, where their big slicing teeth are.

There's no such thing as a sabre-toothed tiger. It's more accurate to say *Smilodon* is a type of sabre-toothed cat.

VENUS FLYTRAP

ALIVE
~48 MYA–NOW
N AMERICA
CARNIVORE

Plants are all the same, right? Green things, growing in the ground, pretty flowers, not doing much apart from soaking up the sun. Well, not all plants are the same. Some have really impressive moving parts and are able to trap their prey before eating them by dissolving them alive.

Although there are lots of different forms, with various colours and shapes, there is only one species of Venus flytrap. The wild form is a small plant, in which the leaves are loosely arranged in a circle formation of between four and seven leaves, each joined to a short stem sitting beneath the ground. The plant is famous for its spiky jaws, but these 'mouths' are actually specialised parts of the leaves.

The Venus flytrap grows where other plants have trouble surviving, such as in boggy habitats with low levels of nitrogen and phosphorus, which most plants need to grow healthily. It also thrives in areas where there are fires from time to time, which removes a lot of the competition.

The Venus flytrap famously traps insects and spiders, when prey brush against the hairs on the inside of the plant's jaws. Brushing against one hair 'triggers' the trap, which only closes when the prey touches a second hair within the next 20 seconds or so.

When prey struggles within the Venus flytrap jaws, it causes the edges of the jaws to seal together, which makes a stomach. Digestive chemicals then dissolve the food inside, to feed the flytrap.

SARCASTIC FRINGEHEAD

- ALIVE
- ~20–10 MYA–NOW
- NE PACIFIC OCEAN
- CARNIVORE

It would be difficult to find a more confusing name than sarcastic fringehead. This little fish may not be sarcastic, but to attract a mate or scare off competition, it does put on one of the most fearsome and impressive displays in the animal kingdom.

The sarcastic fringehead can be up to 30cm in length. Its body is long and thin, with large pectoral fins on the side and a long fin running all the way down its back. These fish vary in colour from brown to dark grey. The mouth of the male is able to fold out and open up, making it as much as four times wider than when closed. When fully open, the mouth is a mix of vibrant blue and purple, lined with a thick yellow lip and border.

The very wide mouth of the male is used for fighting and for either defending its territory or claiming a good spot from another fringehead. When two sarcastic fringeheads fight, they flash their mouths at each other. If that doesn't work, they come together, each pressing its mouth against the other, before wrestling like this. The winner is the one who bites the other's head first.

Sarcastic fringeheads live in natural holes and burrows. Today, they are often found living inside bottles and other human rubbish, which seems more than a little sad, when you think about it.

DILOPHOSAURUS

(di-lo pho sor-us)

EXTINCT
195.2–183.7 MYA
N AMERICA
CARNIVORE

In the early Jurassic period, *Dilophosaurus* was the largest known land animal in North America and one of the earliest predatory dinosaurs anywhere.

Measuring around 7m long and weighing about 400kg, *Dilophosaurus* was two and a half times the length of a brown bear but roughly the same weight. For its size, *Dilophosaurus* was a lightweight dinosaur. Its head was a bit bigger than you'd expect but was quite delicate. The snout was narrow and the upper jaw had a gap just below the nostril. The teeth were long, thin and curved, and those in the lower jaw were much smaller than those in the upper jaw.

Dilophosaurus had two long crests on its skull which probably had a covering of keratin, the same thing that makes up our hair and fingernails. Scientists are still unsure about the use of these crests. They were too weak for fighting or hunting, but perhaps were used for display to help *Dilophosaurus* find a mate, or to scare away others in territorial displays.

Hollywood films mean that most of us don't know the real *Dilophosaurus*. It's one of the most misunderstood dinosaurs ever, because there is no evidence *Dilophosaurus* had a huge frill or was able to spit venom as shown in films.

CORDYCEPS

(cor-dee seps)

- ALIVE
- 48 MYA–NOW
- EUROPE, ASIA, N AMERICA
- ENTOMOPATHO-GENIC

This is a type of fungi, which hijacks the brain of its victim and controls the way it thinks and moves, before killing it in a way that helps the fungi find more victims.

The *Cordyceps* has two main parts. The first is the body-like structure that grows within its victim's or host's body. It's made up of feathery structures called 'hyphae' ('hi-fee'), and is where digestive chemicals are released to absorb nutrients from the host's body.

The other part is the stalk-like 'stroma', which is a fruiting body. This can grow 4–10cm in height. The stroma is dark brown or black but may be yellow when it first grows.

If the microscopic spores from *Cordyceps* land on the exoskeleton of an invertebrate, such as an ant, they move through the outer shell into the body, where they can begin to alter the new host's behaviour. An infected ant may leave its nest and climb higher, where there is more moisture in the air, which helps the fungus grow. The *Cordyceps* makes the ant bite into a leaf or into a branch, anchoring itself there.

As the ant waits, still alive, *Cordyceps* feeds on its insides, finally killing it. A few days later, the fungus sends the stroma stalk out through the ant's body or even just its head. Finally, more spores are released into the air to infect more unsuspecting victims.

As soon as an ant, cockroach, caterpillar or any other invertebrate is infected by *Cordyceps*, it is 100 per cent deadly.

TITANOBOA

- EXTINCT
- 60–58 MYA
- COLOMBIA
- CARNIVORE

Many people are scared of snakes, but there has only ever been one that was truly terrifying. With a body as thick as an adult human's waist, *Titanoboa* was a prehistoric giant reptile.

Growing to a length of 12–14.3m, *Titanoboa* was huge. It may have weighed as much as 1.5 tonnes, the same as a family-sized car. We do not have an entire skeleton of a *Titanoboa* – only some pentagon-shaped vertebrae (back bones) from the middle section of its body, some ribs, some teeth and parts of the skull have been found.

Titanoboa looked like a very big boa constrictor, and would have been most closely related to those snakes found on Madagascar and some Pacific islands today.

There are two main theories about how and what *Titanoboa* hunted. One is that it ambushed anything close enough to grab and would quite easily have eaten large crocodiles and mammals. The other, which seems better supported by the fossils, is that the skull and teeth were adapted to eating fish and that *Titanoboa* would have hunted fish, such as the substantial prehistoric lungfish and relatives of the giant arapaima alive today.

Fifty-eight million years ago, a few million years after the fall of the dinosaurs, Cerrejón in Colombia was an immense, swampy jungle where everything was hotter, wetter and bigger than it is today. The trees had wider leaves, indicating greater rainfall – more than 380cm per year, compared with 200cm in the Amazon now.

PLIOSAUR

(pli-o sor)

- EXTINCT
- 203–66 MYA
- WORLDWIDE OCEANS
- CARNIVORE

The pliosaur was part of a group of marine predatory reptiles which dominated many prehistoric ocean ecosystems. They were fast, powerful and deadly.

Different species were different sizes, ranging from 4m in length to over 10m. All had a short neck, with a long, triangular and slightly flattened skull. One fossilised skull measured 2.85m from front to back. A pliosaur had two pairs of flippers, with the back set larger than the front. It had a mouthful of sharp, cone-shaped teeth. The biggest pliosaurs weighed as much as 15 tonnes, nearly twice the weight of the largest orcas alive today.

It appears to have eaten most things, with smaller fish, sharks, dinosaurs and other marine reptiles such as turtles, ichthyosaurs and even smaller pliosaurs all on the menu. Part of the reason it was able to do this was because of its powerful jaws. We measure force in Newtons (N): humans have a maximum bite force of about 770 N and 100–150 for chewing, but the bigger pliosaurs had a bite force as high as 23,000 N, around 30 times more than ours.

One of the scariest things for a scuba diver is something called 'the bends', caused by rising in the water too quickly after a dive. Changing pressure forms tiny bubbles in the bloodstream, which can be fatal. Some pliosaur fossils show that they also had this condition, maybe from chasing prey, or being chased themselves.

HELICOPRION

(hel-ee co priy-on)

EXTINCT
290–270 MYA
ANCIENT OCEANS
CARNIVORE

This ancient shark-like fish was a huge, fast-swimming predator found in most oceans. It had a unique whorl of teeth, which puzzled scientists for years.

Like its modern-day relatives, sharks, rays and chimaeras (or rat fish), *Helicoprion* had a skeleton made from cartilage (the same bendy stuff as in your nose), which does not fossilise very well. With no fossils from the actual bodies of *Helicoprion*, we have to look at its modern relatives, some ancient fish of which there are fossils, and its teeth, to build a picture of what the body was really like. Scientists think *Helicoprion* grew to between 5–8m in length, similar to a basking shark, but was much faster.

It's most likely *Helicoprion* had a streamlined, torpedo-shaped body, with triangular pectoral fins on its sides. The tail was probably forked, with each part being equal length, telling us something about the way this shark moved and hunted.

Unlike the tails seen on thresher sharks or great whites, *Helicoprion's* forked tail was similar to that of a mako shark or tuna. This type of tail, plus its long body shape, means *Helicoprion* was an active predator, which hunted in open water, like mako sharks, swordfish or tuna.

The whorl could hold as many as 50 serrated teeth, each growing up to 10cm in length.

MOSQUITO

ALIVE
99 MYA-NOW
WORLDWIDE
MALE: HERBIVORE
FEMALE: OMNIVORE

Despite being responsible for the deaths of nearly one million people around the world each year, the 3,600 species of mosquitoes are fascinating flies. They are important for many ecosystems, either by helping pollinate plants or as food for the many, many predators that eat them.

Most mosquitoes are between 3–6mm long and are grey or black in colour. They have a single pair of wings, with a span of 2.8–4.4mm. There are some bigger species though, reaching 18mm in length and 24mm from wingtip to wingtip.

Some mosquitoes can fly non-stop for four hours at speeds between 1–2km/h and can travel up to 12km in a night, maybe on the hunt for blood. All mosquitoes drink nectar from flowers, but the females from some species also drink blood (from vertebrates and invertebrates) to help either produce eggs or to make more eggs.

When flying, a mosquito can beat its wings up to 600 times per second.

Have you ever been in hospital for an operation? Well, if so, there's a chance your life may have been saved by an animal that looks more than a little alien.

The rounded body looks a little bit like a horseshoe and is separated into two main parts, covered by a large protective shell. At the back end is a long, tail-like spine, which is moveable and has a range of functions. In total, a horseshoe crab has six pairs of limbs. Some are used for feeding, some for gripping, and others for walking.

Mostly, the horseshoe crab eats worms and shellfish living on the seabed. It may also feed on crabs and their relatives and even some fish.

In the breeding season, over 250,000 horseshoe crabs can gather on a single beach. Breeding takes place at high tides around full or new moons.

The horseshoe crab is often caught for its blood, which contains special cells like our white blood cells. These can be harvested and used in hospitals to detect whether equipment is properly clean, saving millions of us from dangerous infections.

TOP

Horseshoe crabs are not crabs at all. They're not even part of the crustacean group, which includes lobsters, shrimps and krill. They're part of a group more closely related to spiders, ticks and scorpions.

HORSESHOE CRAB

ALIVE
250 MYA–NOW
ATLANTIC & INDO-PACIFIC OCEANS
CARNIVORE

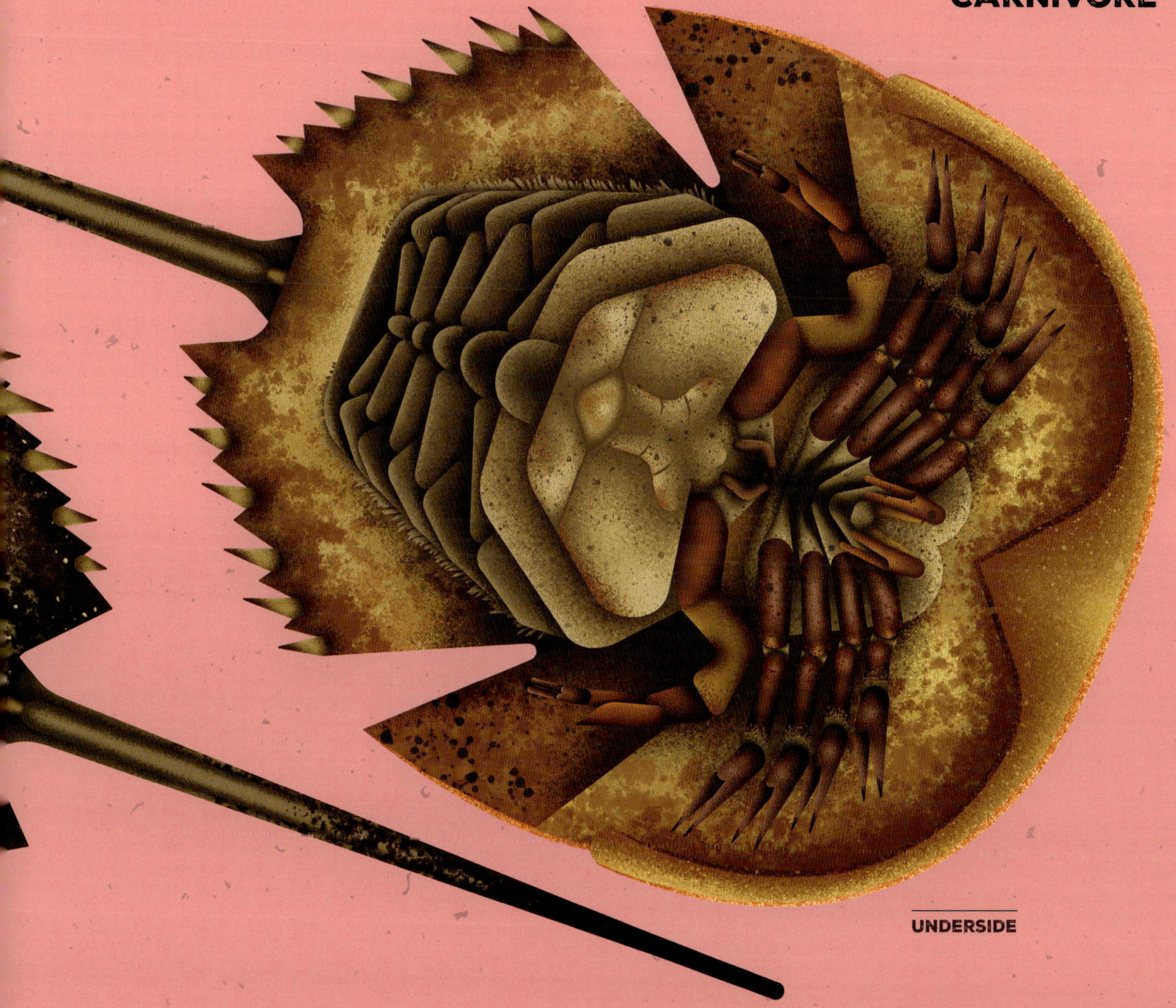

UNDERSIDE

NAKED MOLE-RAT

♥ ALIVE
~20 MYA–NOW
E AFRICA
OMNIVORE

If you think of the ultimate animal – one that doesn't get sick, grows old very, very slowly and can survive in extreme environments, you probably wouldn't imagine a pink, nearly hairless and almost-blind underground rodent, would you?

The naked mole-rat is the only mammal to have a body temperature that goes up and down as the temperature around it changes. If you're wondering, yours stays constant. Apparently, the naked mole-rat does not feel pain through its skin in the way we do. It does not get diseases and can survive in an environment where the amount of oxygen in the air drops from 21 per cent to 2 per cent (which would kill humans in minutes).

A naked mole-rat can live for over 37 years, which is longer than any other rodent. A house mouse might be lucky to live two to three years. Naked mole-rats live in an unusual community, with a queen and one or two males that mate. All the other members of the community (usually between 40 and 70 animals) are workers and only serve the queen.

A naked mole-rat's lips seal behind its teeth, which allows it to dig tunnels with its long, chisel teeth.

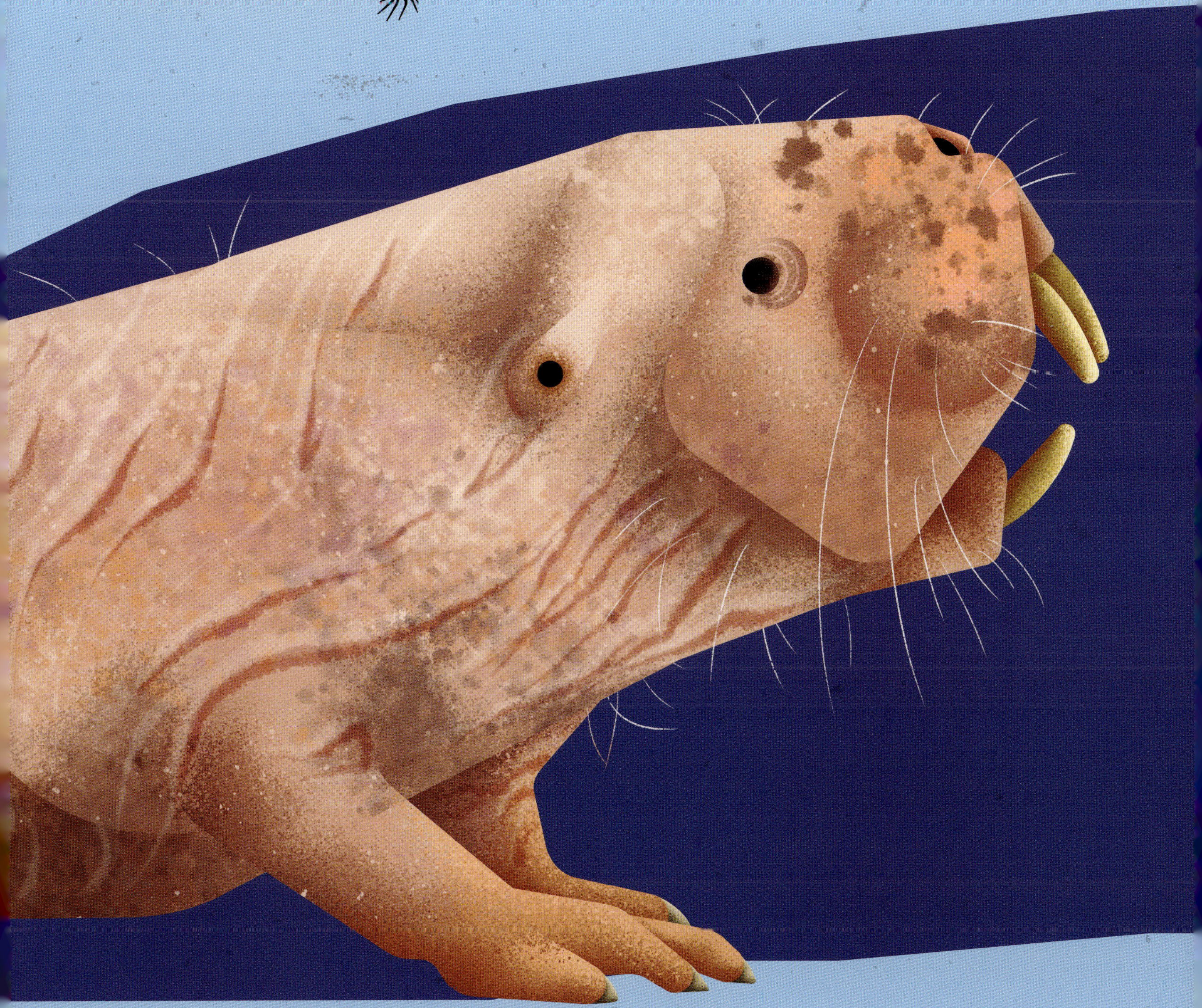

TERROR BIRD

☠ **EXTINCT**
🕓 **43 MYA–17,500 YA**
📍 **N & S AMERICA**
🍴 **CARNIVORE**

Picture a bird, taller than the tallest person you know, that could run almost as fast as a cheetah. Its huge, deadly beak helped make it among the most feared predators in its environment. It deserved its name.

Terror birds ranged from 1–3m tall, and the largest could have weighed as much as four adult humans. It had large sharp claws and a beak measuring up to 46cm in length, which had sharpened edges and an eagle-like hooked tip. Its strong but incredibly flexible neck would have allowed the heavy skull and beak to strike with fatal force and speed. This was not a slow-moving bird, but although it could run fast, the terror bird was flightless.

When scientists studied terror birds, they discovered that despite its dangerous kicking legs and massive beak, its bite force was pretty weak. They assumed these birds would have eaten small animals as prey. But some dinosaurs, like *Allosaurus*, and some sharks, such as the great white, also have a weak bite force *and* a fairly fragile skull, and they definitely eat large prey, so maybe terror birds did go after big animals, after all.

Based on the size, strength and shape of its leg bones, it's possible a terror bird could run as fast as 95 km/h, which is faster than an ostrich and definitely faster than you.

Sometimes in nature, it's not always easy to tell if something is an animal or not. There are examples where an animal looks nothing like an animal, and it can take in-depth investigation to understand how we might be related.

With over 5,000 different species, sponges vary a lot in size and shape. Most are only a few centimetres wide, while others might reach 2m tall. Some look like wide tubes; others are like bunches of fingers, cushions or flat mats, covering rocks. A deep-sea sponge will often be white or brown, whereas in shallow habitats sponges are more brightly coloured: red, yellow, orange, shades of purple and black.

After fertilisation, the sponge larva becomes part of the plankton community, where it is free-swimming for anywhere from a few hours to three or four days. When the larva finds a suitable location, it attaches to a rock or shell and begins turning into a young sponge.

An adult sponge does not have a nervous system, as you might expect in most animals, and its body parts do not move.

Sponges can be found next to the shoreline and as deep as 8,500m beneath the surface. Around 98 per cent are found in marine environments and seem to favour cold, Antarctic waters.

SEA SPONGE

ALIVE
544 MYA–NOW
WORLDWIDE OCEANS
OMNIVORE

The sponge has an amazing ability to regenerate. In a particularly mean set of experiments, sponges were squeezed through fine silk cloth to turn them into a 'mush'. Incredibly, the cells then settled, moved around and reformed a new sponge.

A female saiga antelope will usually give birth to twins.

It's big and round and not far from the ground. It has one of the most famous noses in the animal kingdom.

The saiga is not a big antelope, measuring only around 70cm tall to the shoulder and weighing as much as a very large dog. There were once vast herds, numbered in the millions, before they were heavily hunted by humans, starting in prehistoric times but continuing into the twentieth century.

The very large, round fleshy nose hangs over the mouth and points downwards. The bone structure inside the nose is incredibly complex. Scientists believe the unusual nose helps warm up cold winter air inside the nose and may filter out dust from summer sand and dust storms.

Saiga antelope can travel over 1,000km during their migrations each year, when they form huge groups. Saiga antelope are hunted by wolves and foxes, golden eagles and even ravens, as well as by humans.

SAIGA ANTELOPE

- ALIVE
- 100,000 YA–NOW
- KAZAKHSTAN, RUSSIA
- HERBIVORE

COBRA LILY

♥ ALIVE
🕒 ~36 MYA–NOW
📍 N AMERICA
🍴 CARNIVORE

This carnivorous plant has never existed alongside a cobra, but it looks similar to its menacing namesake.

It has slender, tube-shaped leaves that rise into what looks like a cobra's hood. It even has a smaller leaf with a split end, resembling a cobra's forked tongue.

The cobra lily can survive in conditions which would kill many other types of carnivorous plants, where the habitat dries out for a few months a year.

The cobra lily does not trap rainwater in its pitcher but controls the level of water inside by releasing or absorbing water that has been pumped up from its roots into the trap. A special chemical is added to the water that helps dissolve and digest prey that falls into the watery trap. The walls inside the trap are slippery and have hairs, both of which stop any prey from escaping.

To confuse prey and prevent their escape, the hood of the cobra lily has lots of dead-ends, meaning there's almost no chance anything can find the right way out.

EPIDEXIPTERYX

(eppi-dex ipp-ter-ix)

EXTINCT
164 MYA
CHINA
CARNIVORE

Long ago, a small, pigeon-sized dinosaur was the first animal to use feathers for display and for showing off. From there, all the bright and patterned feathers we see in birds today developed.

This was one of the smallest dinosaurs ever, weighing about the same as two hamsters. It measured just 25cm in length, but its tail feathers, which looked like long streamers, would have doubled this length. These feathers looked more like ribbons than the feathers we know today.

Its skull was unusual, because *Epidexipteryx* only had teeth at the front of its mouth. The teeth were big, considering the dinosaur was so small, and they pointed outwards to help catch prey.

Some scientists believe *Epidexipteryx* could glide, using flaps of skin, but it could not fly like a bird. It had feathers across its body, and hunted by climbing trees and running through the branches catching insects.

So far, we only have one fossil for *Epidexipteryx*.

Imagine being incredibly shy but being labelled 'the world's most dangerous bird'. The three species of cassowary are mysterious and elusive, yet they are fearsome giant, flightless, forest birds.

In the top three for both the tallest bird on Earth and the heaviest living bird, cassowaries are able to reach a height of 1.9m and weigh 85kg, which is about the same height and weight as a very tall and athletic human.

The cassowary has three toes on each foot, all with sharp claws, but the first toe on each side has a dagger-like claw, over 12cm long. It uses this to fight and defend itself with deadly kicks.

On the top of the head sits a bony ridge, with a covering of keratin (the same material that makes up our fingernails). We don't know for certain what this is for, but ideas range from it being used to swish through the thick forest, or to clear leaves to hunt for food on the ground. It might be for displaying to other cassowaries or in fights for dominance. Other ideas are that it may be a way to store or dump heat, or it might be used to help carry the cassowary's booming call further through the forest. The cassowary call is so low, it can barely be heard by humans.

CASSOWARY

(kas-uh wair-ee)

ALIVE
5 MYA–NOW
AUSTRALASIA
OMNIVORE

The cassowary is different to most birds because it does not have a tongue.

THERIZINOSAURUS

(theer-iz inno sor-us)

EXTINCT
70 MYA
MONGOLIA
HERBIVORE

We're often told that being weird isn't a good thing, but to a scientist, being weird means something is even more interesting. One of the most interesting dinosaurs ever described is definitely among the weirdest.

If you combine the large gut of a gorilla, the mouth of a horse and the claws of a sloth, then add bird feathers, you're on your way to recreating one of the most mysterious yet fascinating dinosaurs ever. *Therizinosaurus* was massive compared to its relatives, growing up to 9–10m long, 4–5m tall and weighing possibly over 5 tonnes, about the same as a big African elephant.

Therizinosaurus was a big, slow-moving dinosaur and although it belonged to the group containing many famous meat-eaters like *Tyrannosaurus*, *Spinosaurus* and *Velociraptor*, this theropod was a herbivore. It most likely ate leaves from bushes and trees. *Therizinosaurus* had the longest claws of any animal ever, reaching up to 50cm in length. That's longer than your arm. Scientists are still not sure what they were used for. Some have suggested they were for digging or for pulling down branches to reach edible leaves. Others think they were for fighting off predators. Perhaps *Therizinosaurus* used them for display, showing off how impressive it was.

When *Therizinosaurus* fossils were first found, scientists believed they were from a giant sea turtle and the claws were from huge flippers.

GIRAFFE BEETLE

ALIVE
~150 MYA–NOW
MADAGASCAR
HERBIVORE

In nature, males from all sorts of species fight, using antlers, horns, brightly coloured feathers and immense size to win. But in the forests of Madagascar, brightly coloured little beetles wrestle using their extraordinary long necks.

The giraffe beetle is about 30mm long, approximately the length of your thumb. It has a black body and bright red wing coverings. It's best known for its very long neck, which gives it its name and is two or three times longer in males than in females.

Scientists think this beetle uses its long neck for fighting, attracting mates and to help with feeding and even building nests.

When trying to impress a mate, a male sways and swishes his neck to show off his bright colours. The female will be watching and, if she thinks his dancing is good enough, they'll mate.

Giraffe beetles spend almost their entire lives on or around a single type of tree, known as the giraffe beetle tree, where they eat the leaves, or maybe the sap from the leaves.

DEINOTHERIUM

(dino-theer ee-um)

EXTINCT
14–1 MYA
AFRICA, EUROPE, ASIA
HERBIVORE

Although fossils show that *Deinotherium* did have a trunk, scientists do not think it looked like the trunks seen in elephants today. It may have been shorter and more muscular.

When natural climate change turned forests into open grasslands across Africa, it caused the extinction of a group of ancient relatives of our modern elephants.

This ancient elephant relative was over a metre taller and more than twice the weight of the biggest African elephants alive today. It measured over 4m high at the shoulder and weighed over 13 tonnes. Overall, it did look a lot like living elephants but had a much more flexible neck and downward-growing, backward-pointing tusks. The legs would have been longer and thinner than those we see now on elephants.

This giant mammal was a herbivore and browsed the branches of trees and bushes across its forest habitat. Its downward-facing tusks were not used for digging or for attracting mates, leaving scientists to believe they were used to help feeding.

The deepest parts of the oceans are cold and dark and the pressure is high enough to crush your body. It's a scary, lonely place but something nightmarish hunts down there . . .

There are many types of deep-sea anglerfish. They vary in size, shape and colour. Some are so grey they are almost black, others are red-brown. Some are 2–3cm long but others can reach 1m. Every deep-sea species has a massive, semi-circular mouth, lined with inward-facing, fang-like teeth, so that once something is caught, there's no escape. They all also have a special fin ray, which can be twitched or wiggled. At the tip is a special type of bacteria that produces light, attracting fish, squid and other animals towards the anglerfish's mouth.

Finding a mate in such a hostile environment is difficult, so to increase their chances of reproducing, the males of some species do something unusual. The male is smaller than the female, and when they meet, it bites the larger female and hangs on. Over time, though scientists don't yet know how long, the male's body dissolves into the female, so that almost nothing is left. A single female can have lots of half-dissolved parasite males attached.

DEEP-SEA ANGLERFISH

ALIVE

50 MYA–NOW

WORLDWIDE OCEANS

CARNIVORE

The anglerfish's bones are thin and flexible and it can distend both its jaw and stomach to an enormous size, allowing it to swallow prey twice as large as its entire body.

DUNG CANNON

ALIVE

~240 MYA–NOW

WORLDWIDE

SAPROTROPH (sap-ro tro-ph)

The dung cannon is a fungus. It does not photosynthesise, turning light energy from the sun into food energy, like plants, and it does not directly eat its food, like animals. Instead, it lives on or inside its food, releasing chemicals to dissolve the food to gain nutrients it then absorbs.

Although this fungus only grows to be 2–4cm tall, it can shoot little capsules, which contain its spores, up to 2m away. This is the equivalent of you throwing a football further than a whole pitch. The spores are microscopic particles which act like seeds in plants, allowing the fungi to reproduce.

This unusual fungus fixes its spores to grass and leaves, which get eaten by cows. The spores pass through the cows' gut and grows only on their poo.

As the little spore capsule is shot off, it travels at 0–70km/h. This is the same g-force (which is the way we measure the forces involved when something accelerates and how gravity affects it) as an incredible 20,000g. To put this in perspective, a really fast roller-coaster might hit 5g. Any more and you'd pass out!

AYE-AYE

ALIVE
25-30 MYA-NOW
MADAGASCAR
CARNIVORE

There's an animal so feared by some people that they believe if you see one, and it points its long, bony finger towards you, you will die.

The aye-aye is a nocturnal lemur, with a body about 60cm in length and a longer thick, brushy tail. It is dark brown or black, with large, forward-facing eyes and big, sensitive ears. It has rodent-like teeth, which are constantly growing, and a special thin, clawed middle finger to hook grubs and larvae from tree trunks.

An aye-aye spends about 80 per cent of the night looking for food. It taps on branches and logs eight times per second and listens for the echo of a hollow chamber beneath. Using its teeth like chisels, it makes a hole, then reaches in with its clawed finger to explore the hole and extract any tasty grubs.

The name aye-aye may come from the Madagascan phrase for 'I don't know', as people may have wanted to avoid talking about an animal they were so scared of.

POTOO

(pot-oo)

ALIVE
48 MYA–NOW
CENTRAL & S AMERICA
CARNIVORE

Camouflage is the art of blending in to look like something else, so you are not seen. There are lots of possible winners for 'best camouflage' award, but one little bird uses its appearance and behaviour to blend perfectly with its surroundings, making it nature's ultimate hide-and-seek winner.

A potoo is 21–58cm in length and looks similar to nightjars and frogmouths. For its body size, the potoo has long wings and a big head. It has been described as being 'little more than a flying mouth and eyes'. Its bill is wide but not long. A notch on either side of the upper bill that looks and acts like a tooth may be used to search for food.

Its feathers are a combination of mottled colours, which helps it blend against the rough bark and tree stumps in its forest habitat.

While adults are camouflaged to look like dead tree stumps, the young potoo is pale, even white in places, and blends in by looking like little clumps of fungi.

The potoo is strictly nocturnal, only flying and hunting at night. It spends most of the daytime staying safe, blending in with branches or resembling a tree stump.

Unlike your best efforts to pretend you're suddenly frozen solid, when the potoo senses danger, it turns into a living statue. It does this so slowly you can barely see it moving, then it settles into position, tail down and head up. It can stay like this for hours and hours.

BLUE DRAGON

- ALIVE
- ~180 MYA–NOW
- INDIAN, PACIFIC & ATLANTIC OCEANS
- CARNIVORE

Think of a slug. Now paint it with blue stripes, add lots of strange-looking swimming 'fingers' and drop it in the middle of the ocean. Give your slug an appetite for some of the most deadly marine organisms, which will help keep it safe from predators.

This little swimming sea slug is about 3cm long and is different shades of blues and greys. It has a flat body, narrowing towards the tail end. There are six points, called 'peduncles', running along either side of its body. These branch into as many as 84 long structures resembling thin fingers.

The blue dragon takes gulps of air, filling its stomach and making it float. Because of where its tummy is, it floats on its back, meaning its upper side, on the surface of the water, is actually its foot.

When hungry, a blue dragon swims towards prey and starts eating with its small but strong jaws and sharp, serrated teeth. It eats a range of prey in the open oceans, but it appears to especially enjoy a lethal meal, with the venomous Portuguese man o' war at the top of the menu. Not only is a blue dragon immune to the man o' war's stinging cells, but it can store them, to use defensively.

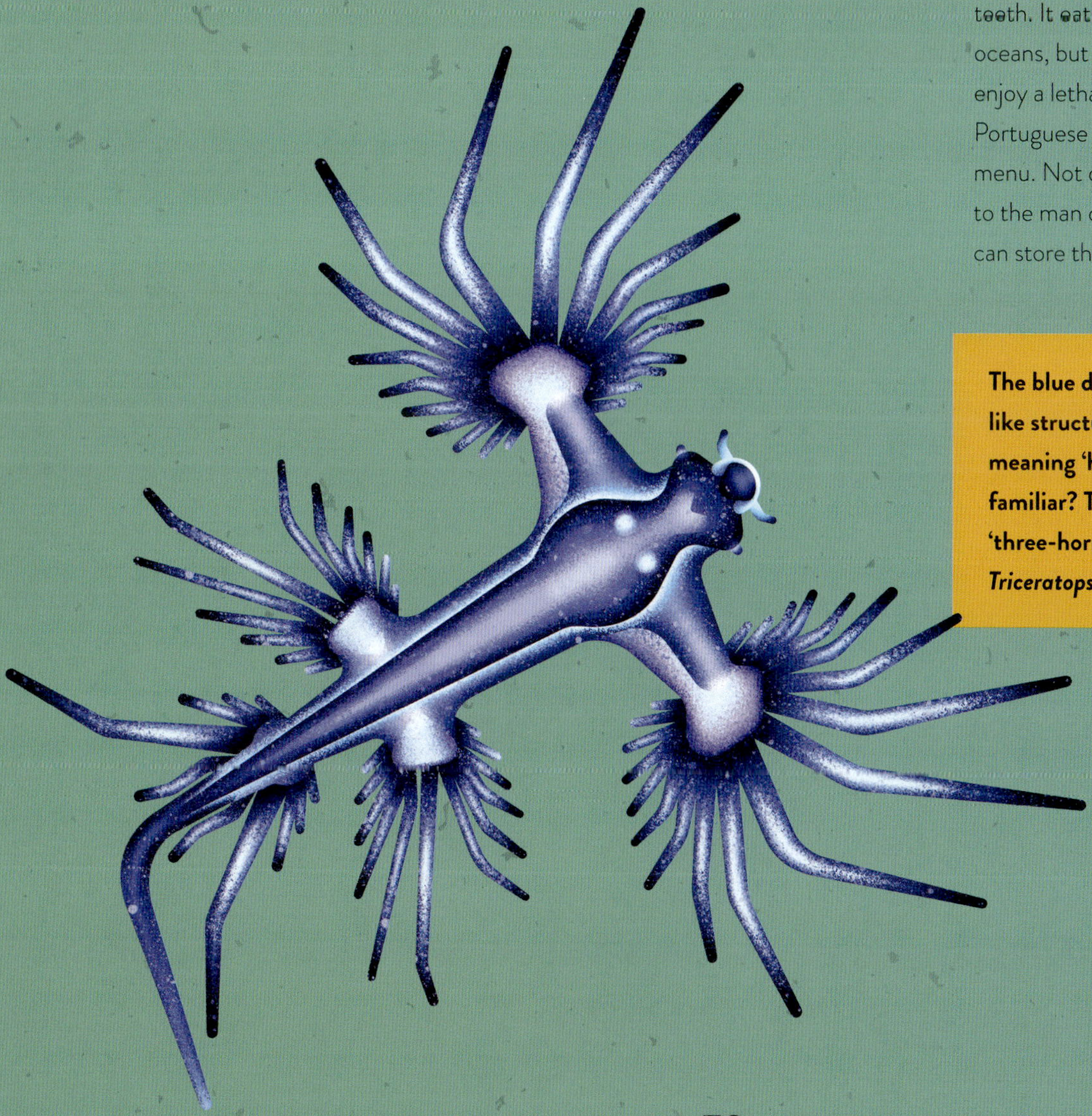

The blue dragon's little finger-like structures are called 'cerata', meaning 'horn' in Greek. Sound familiar? Think of that famous 'three-horned' dinosaur, *Triceratops*.

QUETZALCOATLUS

(kwet-zal co-at luss)

EXTINCT
68–66 MYA
N AMERICA
CARNIVORE

What do you know about the way reptiles move? A snake slithers. A lizard runs. A crocodile swims. Some ancient reptiles moved in surprising ways and were in fact the largest animals ever to fly.

The bird with the largest wings today is the wandering albatross, with a wingspan of 3.7m. With a wingspan over two and a half times bigger, at 10m, *Quetzalcoatlus* was the biggest flying animal ever. It was as tall as a giraffe, about 5m, and as heavy as a pygmy hippo, about 270kg.

Piecing together ancient animal behaviour is never easy, and with only a few fossils, *Quetzalcoatlus* is quite a prehistoric puzzle. Was it a scavenger or did it skim fish from the water? It's likely it spent its days hunting and catching animals such as small reptiles, mammals and even dinosaurs.

Scientists are far from certain, but some studies hint that *Quetzalcoatlus* may have been able to fly non-stop for days and for thousands of kilometres.

Belonging to a group related to slugs and snails, the cuttlefish is unlike its slimy cousins; it is a fast, venomous, shape-shifting, colour-changing genius.

There are different species of cuttlefish, ranging from 5–50cm long. The largest weighs over 10kg, the smallest less than a chicken egg. All have eight arms and two tentacles with suckers for catching prey. Unlike octopus and squid, a cuttlefish has a special structure *inside* its body called a cuttlebone. It's easy to think of it as a skeleton, but, changing the amount of liquid and gas within the cuttlebone, helps the cuttlefish float or sink. Its w-shaped pupils give it amazing vision, although it cannot see in colour.

If you compare the size of its brain to the overall size of its body, the cuttlefish is more impressive than almost any other invertebrate, supporting the idea that it is one of the most intelligent invertebrates on the planet. Cuttlefish communicate with each other and other animals by using over 50 different signals. When chased, the cuttlefish produces a cloud of ink that acts as a smokescreen, allowing it to escape.

Some research has shown that cuttlefish brains may be so developed, they are able to dream. Scientists are still not sure what they might be dreaming about. Yet.

CUTTLEFISH

- ALIVE
- ~70 MYA–NOW
- SOME TROPICAL & TEMPERATE OCEANS
- CARNIVORE

There was a dinosaur-sized armadillo that lived across South America thousands of years ago. It had a huge bony shell that made it almost invincible to predators.

With its large, rounded dome-like shell and weighing up to 2 tonnes, the *Glyptodon* was about the same size, shape, and weight as a Volkswagen Beetle car, but a bit longer. It measured up to 3.5m from nose to tail tip. The shell was made up from around 1,800 flat bony structures called 'osteoderms' (oss tee o derms), which were shaped like hexagons, all fitting together.

So far, we can't say whether or not *Glyptodon* lived in groups. From tell-tale injuries and damage seen on fossils, it does seem that when they met, there was often a lot of fighting. The tail was used as a weapon. It was flexible and the hard bony rings could cause a lot of harm. Some fossils show damage to the protective shells, which scientists think might have been caused by these fights.

GLYPTODON

(glip-tow don)

EXTINCT
3.2 MYA-11,000 YA
S AMERICA
HERBIVORE

Due to its armour-plating, *Glyptodon* did not have many enemies, but sabre-toothed cats, jaguars and the terror bird were among its predators.

PAKICETUS

(pa-kee see-tus)

EXTINCT
50–48 MYA
PAKISTAN
CARNIVORE

Whales are instantly recognisable ... big things ... really big things, in fact. No legs. Live in water. Probably eat krill. But there was once a small whale that lived on the land, walked around on four legs and hunted in and out of the water. It was the first whale.

Weighing around 45kg, about the same as ten large pet cats, *Pakicetus* measured between 1-2m long. It had a long skull and different types of teeth, such as incisors, canines, premolars and molars, all adapted for eating meat. Although this four-legged carnivore didn't look like a modern whale, its skull gives us several clues as to its real nature. Fossils show the inner ear was protected by a bony casing, which we see in whales alive today, but in no other mammal. Its jaws also show that its way of hearing was more like that of mammals living on land than those living in water. Unlike whales today, its neck was very flexible.

Some researchers believe *Pakicetus* spent almost all its time on land, others think it spent a lot of time in water. Different parts of its skeleton support each idea. The thickened wall of bone around its inner ear is seen in all whales and helps them hear underwater, but sound actually reached the inner ear through the ear canal, just like it does in you and every other land animal.

Most scientists agree *Pakicetus* can be seen as the first whale even though it looked more like a wolf, and would have been most closely related to hippopotamuses.

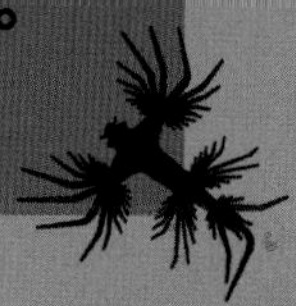

If you eat a carrot, you don't genetically become a little bit of carrot, but amazingly, this is what *Rafflesia* does. It takes on some of the DNA from its host plant and mixes it into its own genetic recipe.

RAFFLESIA

(raff-l eez ee-a)

ALIVE
55–50 MYA–NOW
ASIA
PARASITE

One of the most specialised parasites in nature, the 'stinking corpse lily' is a plant with no stem, no leaves and no roots. It has what might be the largest flower on Earth.

There are maybe as many as 40 (or more) different species of *Rafflesia*. Flowers can measure an incredible 120cm wide and weigh 10kg (or as much as a small dog, such as a sausage dog). The flower has five giant petals, usually in shades of red or orange, with yellow spots.

The flowers look and smell like rotting flesh. This disgusting odour is irresistible to many insects, which are attracted to the flowers in search of a meal. Instead, they end up transporting pollen from male to female flowers, helping them reproduce. *Rafflesia* grows on only two or three specific types of vine and these vines grow on other plants, so it's fair to think of it as a parasite on a parasite.

VAMPIRE FINCH

♥ ALIVE
🕒 500,000 YA–NOW
📍 GALÁPAGOS ISLANDS
🍴 OMNIVORE

Its vampire-like behaviour may have started with picking off parasites from other birds, which would have bled sometimes. Over the last half million years or so, the finch may have evolved to miss out the parasite-picking entirely to focus on getting nutritious blood instead.

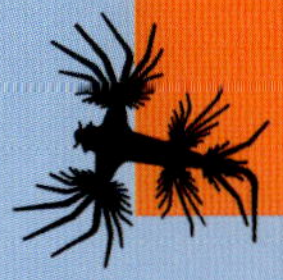

The Galápagos Islands are famous for their finches, which all feed on different things in different ways. Some eat nuts, using powerful, big beaks, and others have sharp, pointed beaks for eating insects. But there's one little bird that drinks the blood of other birds.

Vampire finch males and females look different to each other. Males are small and black, females are grey with brown streaks. Weighing around 20g, a vampire finch is about the same weight as a mouse.

The vampire finch mostly eats seeds and insects but is able to change its diet when food is scarce. It is able to eat eggs, bits of fish left by other predators and even bird poo. But it is most famous for its love of blood. Strangely, when the finch uses its sharp beak to create a cut and begin to drink blood, the victim seems either not to notice or doesn't seem to care too much. The finch seems to focus on much larger birds, such as boobies, and can cause quite large injuries. However, it seems only around ten per cent of a vampire finch's diet is blood.

DUCK-BILLED PLATYPUS

ALIVE

5 MYA–100,000 YA –NOW

AUSTRALIA

CARNIVORE

Think you know mammals? Think again. This one lays eggs, has a venomous spur and is able to sense electricity to hunt prey.

The body and broad, flat tail are covered with dense, brown, waterproof fur that traps a layer of air to help keep the platypus warm. Along with the four echidna species, the platypus is among the few mammals to lay eggs, rather than give birth to live babies.

The male has a small bony spur on each hind foot, which is able to deliver a venom so painful, some unlucky people have said it was 'excruciating' for weeks.

When hunting in cloudy, dark water, the platypus is able to close its eyes, ears and nose. It uses electrolocation to detect tiny electrical signals given off by prey in the water or buried in the mud.

Platypus fur gives off a bluish-green biofluorescent glow when seen under UV light. We have no idea if or how this benefits the platypus. This is an example of how science is always a process of discovery – the more we look, the more we learn.

LAMPREY

ALIVE
360 MYA–NOW
COASTS & RIVERS WORLDWIDE
CARNIVORE

Sometimes it's fun to bend the rules a little, but the lamprey seems to ignore many of the rules of nature that help us understand which group it actually belongs to.

Almost every other vertebrate animal has limbs arranged in pairs, a spinal cord that is protected by a series of backbones made of bone or cartilage and a whole list of other things. The lamprey doesn't have fins in pairs and doesn't have a spinal cord, but something similar called a notochord. It also doesn't have a stomach and doesn't even have jaws. It's a vertebrate, but only just.

A lamprey's long, scale-less body can reach over 1m in length. It has just one nostril and seven pairs of gill pores on either side of its head.

A scavenger, the lamprey eats by attaching its mouthparts to a body, using circular rows of thorny teeth to grab hold. Three horny plates on the tip of its tongue are used to scrape through the surface of the prey until it reaches softer parts beneath. Some lamprey species have evolved to eat flesh, while some eat blood and others wriggle inside the body to eat the organs only.

The lamprey is said to have four eyes but this isn't quite accurate. They have a pair of true eyes and they also have two extra sensory organs, which act a bit like eyes but sense light in a different way.

TARBOSAURUS

(tar-bo sor-us)

EXTINCT
70–68 MYA
MONGOLIA
CARNIVORE

There was once a large, predatory dinosaur with a massive head and around 60 dagger-like teeth. It had small arms and lived during the Cretaceous period, but it wasn't the *Tyrannosaurus rex*.

At over 10m long and weighing around 5 tonnes, or as much as an African elephant, *Tarbosaurus* was a big predator but was still smaller than its more famous North American relative. Its skull measured 135cm long, with a special adaptation in the jaws, not seen in other dinosaurs, that helped them lock into place.

The skull shows us *Tarbosaurus* had a good sense of smell, but poor eyesight. It's also possible to tell that it had good hearing, which it may have used in hunting or to communicate with others of its kind. By looking at the bite marks left on other fossils and by studying the chemicals left in *Tarbosaurus* fossils, we can tell it mainly fed on hadrosaurs and sauropods.

There was a long discussion about whether *Tarbosaurus* and *Tyrannosaurus* were actually the same animal but living in different parts of the world, or if they were completely different. For now, it appears *Tarbosaurus* was different.

AMAZONIA GIANT CENTIPEDE

- ALIVE
- 2.5 MYA–NOW
- S AMERICA
- CARNIVORE

There are many things in tropical forests that can either bite or sting. As the largest of its kind in the world, the Amazonia giant centipede is a dangerous predator, hunting through the forests of South America.

This sizeable invertebrate can reach a length of over 30cm. Its body is made up of 21–23 individual segments, each with a pair of legs attached. Like all centipedes, it can deliver a painful sting, injecting venom through its specially adapted legs called 'toxicognaths' (tox-ik-o nathes) rather than fangs.

The Amazonia giant centipede is an active hunter and will eat insects, worms, snails, small spiders and millipedes. It will also tackle more dangerous and much bigger prey. It has been known to kill and eat scorpions and tarantulas, as well as frogs, small lizards and snakes, mice and even some species of bird.

Some very large centipedes specialise in hunting bats by climbing up to the roof of a cave where the bats roost. Gripping with a few pairs of legs, the centipede will catch, overpower and eat its flying prey. It does have its own predators and is hunted by birds, giant tarantulas and mammals such as coatis and kinkajous.

Despite having the name centipede, which means 'one hundred legs', no species found so far has exactly this number. Some have fewer, others have more.

HOATZIN

(ho-at zin)

ALIVE
10-5 MYA–NOW
S AMERICA
FOLIVORE

Many animals have more than one name, often based on what is known about them. For the hoatzin it's the 'stink bird'. The 'stink' comes from a combination of chemicals in the leaves the bird eats and the smelly bacteria that breaks down the leaves.

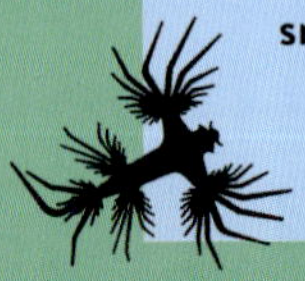

The hoatzin is around 65cm long, about the same size as a pheasant. It has a blue face and dark red eyes. Its small head is featherless, but brown feathers cover the rest of its body, with a green-bronze band across its tail.

More than 80 per cent of the hoatzin's diet is leaves. The rest includes more than 50 different species of plants, flowers and fruit. A hoatzin's gut, like a cow's, contains specialist bacteria that break down tough plant material. This is very unusual in a bird and means that scientists still find exactly how the hoatzin relates to other birds a bit of a mystery.

A hoatzin chick has two claws on each wing. Straight after hatching, it uses these claws and its big feet to scrabble through branches without falling into the water in its swamp home. But if it is threatened by a predator, it drops into the water and swims away, then uses its strange claws to climb back to safety.

The hoatzin is noisy, making a variety of croaking, hissing and grunting sounds. Because the bird smells so bad, it is rarely hunted by humans. If it is eaten, its meat can be toxic to us.

SARCOSUCHUS

(sar-ko soo-cus)

EXTINCT
133–112 MYA
AFRICA, S AMERICA
CARNIVORE

An ancient relative of crocodiles alive today, *Sarcosuchus*, meaning the 'flesh crocodile', was among the largest prehistoric predators ever.

Both species of the giant *Sarcosuchus* looked like modern crocodiles, in particular the gharial. *Sarcosuchus* was huge, measuring up to 9.5m in length and weighing between 3 to 4.5 tonnes, similar to an African elephant. Some scientists believe *Sarcosuchus* may even have weighed twice this much.

Its long, slender snout made up 75 per cent of the skull's total length, with 35 teeth in each side of its upper jaw and 31 in each side of its lower jaw. The upper jaw was noticeably longer than the lower. Its eyes appear to have been set in little turrets, like telescopes.

Because the skull looks similar to that of the fish-eating gharial, some scientists believe *Sarcosuchus* also ate fish. Others think it may have hunted and killed much larger animals including dinosaurs. There were lots of dinosaurs, such as iguanodons, hadrosaurs, sauropods and theropods, living alongside *Sarcosuchus*. Research has shown that *Sarcosuchus* was not able to do the 'death roll' like crocodiles today, which may have affected how it killed prey.

Although there is no fossil evidence, it's possible that *Sarcosuchus* and the huge fish-eating dinosaur *Spinosaurus* lived alongside each other and may have met. We may never know if they met and if they did, who would have won a fight.

SHOEBILL

- ALIVE
- ~20 MYA–NOW
- AFRICA
- CARNIVORE

It's often clear to see how birds and extinct dinosaurs are related, but there are some birds where it's really obvious! The shoebill could easily have been at home hunting baby dinosaurs in prehistoric swamps.

The shoebill is a very tall, long-legged wading bird. Most reach a height of 110–140cm, but some reach 152cm. The wingspan can measure 260cm across, about the same as the height of a room in your home. It weighs 4–7kg, the weight of a small dog. An adult shoebill is shades of grey, while the young are brown.

The name comes from the bird's massive bill. Long and wide, it has a sharp hooked tip and can reach 24cm in length. Only pelicans and large storks have longer bills.

The shoebill is described as being like a statue, which is pretty accurate, as it stands for hours barely moving, waiting for the right moment to strike. The shoebill is generally silent, but the adult performs displays, clattering its huge bill around nests. It can make high-pitched whining sounds and when it does call, it is said to make a cow-like 'moo'.

A shoebill eats fish, including lungfish, tilapia and catfish, along with frogs, snakes, monitor lizards, small mammals and other birds. It will even eat baby crocodiles, if it has the chance.

The shoebill's scientific name *Balaeniceps rex* means 'whale head' because the head is so big and so unusual for a bird.

RED KANGAROO

ALIVE
2 MYA–NOW
AUSTRALIA
HERBIVORE

Reaching speeds of up to 60km/h and able to cover over 9m in a single leap, the red kangaroo is one of nature's greatest athletes.

The largest of all kangaroos and the largest living marsupial (pouched mammals), the red kangaroo is also the largest native land mammal alive in Australia. Males grow to a height of 1.6m, with a 1.2m tail. Females are smaller, usually 85–105cm tall, with a tail length of 65–85cm. Females generally weigh 18–40kg; males twice as much, at 55–90kg.

The red kangaroo has two forelimbs with small claws and two muscular hind limbs for jumping. Its strong tail creates a tripod for support when standing upright and walking or for balance when jumping.

The female red kangaroo has a pouch, where she keeps developing embryos and later slightly older young (called joeys). A baby red kangaroo emerges after only 33 days of developing. Blind, hairless and the size of a jelly bean, it uses its well-developed forelimbs and claws to climb towards the pouch for food and safety. After approximately 190 days, the joey is strong enough to leave the pouch on its own. It returns to feed, sleep and for safety, but after 235 days or so, the joey will be evicted from its home.

It might not create the same response as 'great white' but, in Australia, adult males are known as 'Big Reds'.

ORCHID MANTIS

- ALIVE
- ~36 MYA–NOW
- SE ASIA
- CARNIVORE

Several species of praying mantis look and behave like orchid flowers, hiding 'in plain sight' until the perfect moment to strike prey with lightning speed. To help it catch food, it sways in the breeze in the same way as a real flower.

Although, like all insects, the orchid mantis has six legs, it only uses four, which resemble orchid petals, to walk. The front pair are adapted into grabbing tools, with a line of long, sharp spines behind a main, curved spike to help grasp and hold prey. The orchid mantis can change colour from brown to bright pink, depending on the colour of the background.

Females are much larger than males. This possibly allows the smaller males a greater chance of escape, as females often try to eat them after mating.

Mantises have great vision and see the world in 3D. Each eye has around 10,000 cell-like structures, which help the mantis pinpoint the exact location of a meal. Slow-motion cameras reveal it can strike at a speed of 60 milliseconds (a millisecond is one-thousandth of a second).

Like all mantises, the orchid mantis has an enormous appetite. It prefers prey from the butterfly and moth group, but also catches flies, fruit flies, beetles, crickets, caterpillars and small species of bees and wasps.

The colours and patterns of the orchid mantis are so convincing that research has found it can attract more insects than actual flowers are able to. This is called aggressive mimicry.

LEAF SHEEP

- ALIVE
- ~100 MYA–NOW
- INDO-PACIFIC OCEAN
- HERBIVORE

Next time you eat a salad, imagine your body could store all the microscopic green bits, which then turned you green and allowed you to sunbathe and turn that sunlight into food for energy. Well, that's exactly what the small sea slug called the leaf sheep does.

The tiny leaf sheep grows up to 10mm in length. It has two dark eyes and two little lumps that look like a cross between horns and ears on its head. These are called rhinophores (ry-no forrs) and they 'smell' chemicals in the water, enabling the leaf sheep to find food.

The leaf sheep eats algae but then does something really special. It sorts out structures in the plants that contain chlorophyll, which captures sunlight, and converts it into useful energy that it stores for itself. Once the leaf sheep has its own store of chlorophyll, it can produce its own energy from sunlight.

Baby leaf sheep hatch from their eggs with tiny shells. They float for a few weeks as plankton, which is the vast mix of small plants and animals floating with the moving water currents through the world's oceans. They then shed their shell and sink down to start life on the reef.

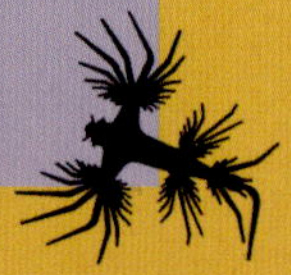

DUNG BEETLE

♥ ALIVE
🕓 53 MYA–NOW
📍 WORLDWIDE
🍴 DETRITIVORE

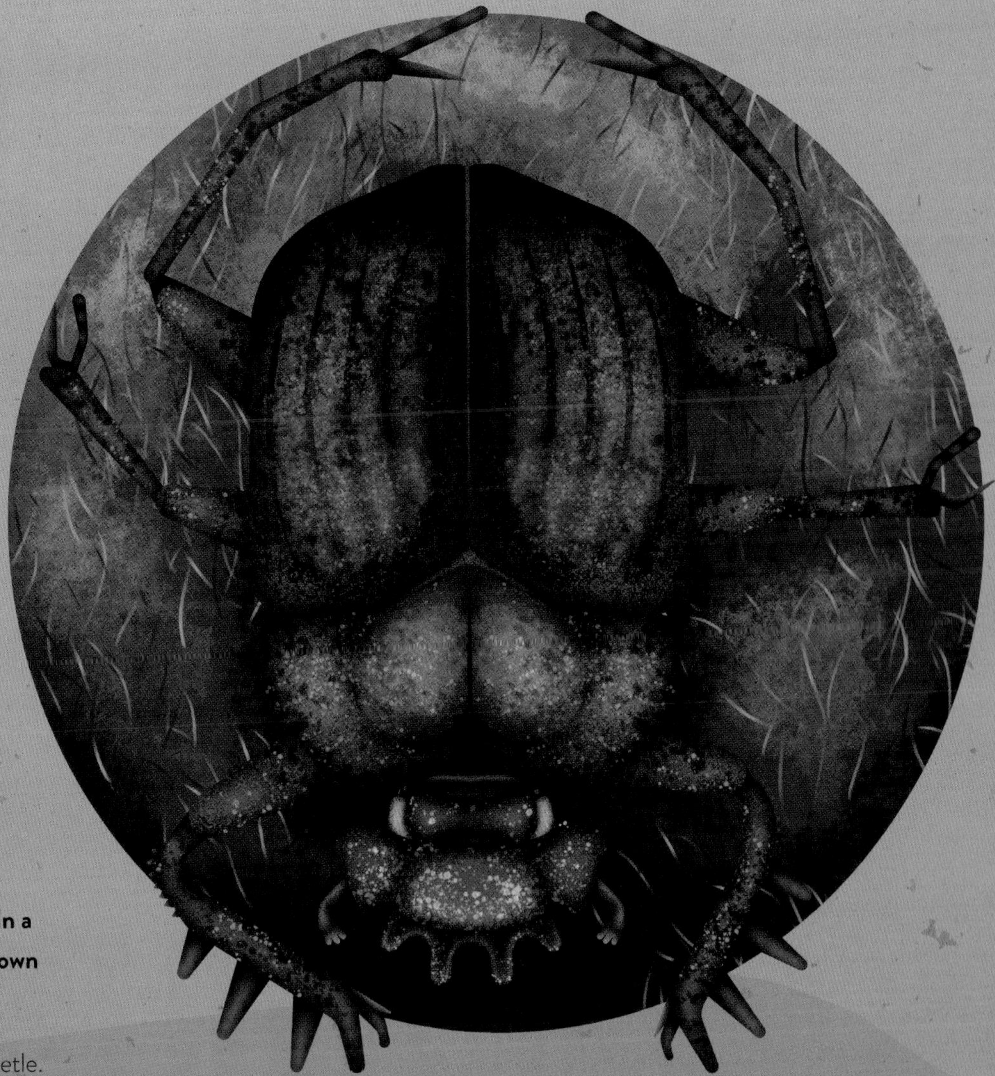

One of the most important and hardworking insects on the planet, the dung beetle specialises in animal poo. In a single night, it can bury 250 times its own body weight of dung.

There are three main groups of dung beetle. They each look a little different, but all have a hard, rounded wing case and often legs with ridges and spikes to help move dung. Rollers make a ball of dung and roll it to a specific place before burying it to eat or use as a breeding chamber. Tunnellers bury dung where it's found. Dwellers don't move the dung at all, but live inside it where they find it, right there on the ground.

A dung beetle plays an important role in changing the structure of soil and improving its nutrient cycle. This means farmers, gardeners and even governments are fans of the dung beetle, as it helps grow more plants and allows seeds to be transported and fertilised. It also prevents diseases spreading between farm animals through the dung by 'hiding' a lot of it under the ground. In some places, such as South Africa, road signs tell drivers to give way to dung beetles on the road.

Some dung beetles use the Milky Way in the night sky to help them find their way around. Only a very small number of invertebrates are able to do this.

The dung produced by one elephant in one day can support a whopping two million dung beetles.

PORTUGUESE MAN O'WAR

ALIVE
~580 MYA–NOW
WORLDWIDE OCEANS
CARNIVORE

Some organisms are made up of countless individual animals, all cooperating to make one biological 'super organism'. The Portuguese man o' war is perhaps the most famous of these colonial organisms and is also known for its venomous sting.

The man o' war belongs to the same group as corals and jellyfish. Its most obvious feature is its gas-filled bladder that sits above the surface of the water. Pink, blue or purple in colour, the bladder is translucent and measures 10–30cm long and 15cm high. The bladder allows the man o' war to float and catch the wind to move it across the ocean.

The man o 'war is equipped with stinging tentacles, which vary in length from 10–30m. Each tentacle is covered in small, thin coiled structures called 'nematocysts' (nee-mat-o sists). On contact with something such as a fish or squid, the nematocysts trigger and inject venom – stinging, paralysing and killing the prey.

A single man o' war is made up from many, many individuals, fully formed smaller organisms called 'zooids' (zoo-ids), which are joined together and share nutrients. Each grows to perform a particular function and although they are separate units, they cannot survive on their own. It's the ultimate example of cooperation.

Named after an 18th-century armed sailing ship, the Portuguese man o' war is also known as the 'bluebottle' and the 'floating terror'.

GIGANTOPITHECUS

(ji-gant-o pith ee-cuss)

EXTINCT
3 MYA–222,000 YA
SE ASIA, CHINA
HERBIVORE

What's the lowest number of fossil bones you'd need to recreate an entire skeleton from an unknown extinct animal? Is only a handful of teeth and the lower jaw enough?

By using measurements from animals alive today, a lot can be told from teeth and lower jaws to help us understand what this giant ape looked like. We may never find anything more because scavengers, such as porcupines, are likely to have eaten anything else before it was fossilised.

Predictions about the height and weight of *Gigantopithecus* have varied massively and will never be certain, unless we find more bones. It was said to be twice the size and weight of an adult male gorilla. A scientist predicted its height at 3.7m. This was later reduced, by another team, to 2.7m tall and weighing 270kg, still around 40 per cent heavier than the average male gorilla. Recently, scientists have settled on the idea that *Gigantopithecus* would have weighed 200–300kg.

Although little of its fossil skeleton has been discovered so far, the teeth reveal a lot about how the animal lived. Scientists were able to look at the chemicals in them, to discover *Gigantopithecus* was a herbivore that ate a range of different fruits, leaves and forest plants.

This giant ape was first discovered by a scientist who happened to be looking through items in a pharmacy in Hong Kong in 1935. Some teeth there were labelled 'dragon bones'. Luckily, he found them before they were used in Chinese remedies.

SEA PEN

ALIVE
500+ MYA–NOW
WORLDWIDE OCEANS
OMNIVORE

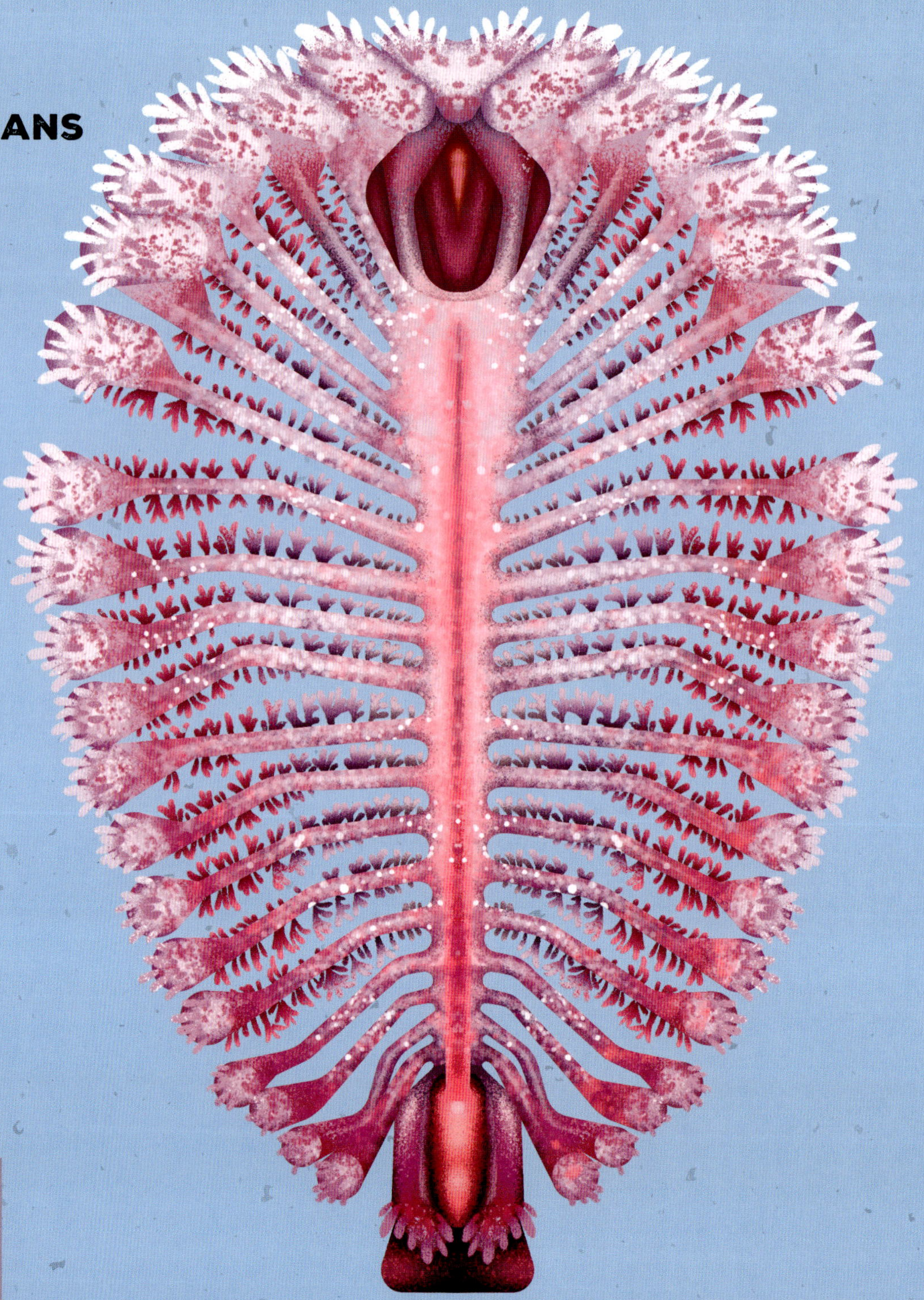

The sea pen looks like a cross between a plant and a giant feather, wafting through the water. It's actually part of the 'animal' category though, and is a colonial animal, where one organism is made up of many smaller, individual organisms, called 'zooids' (zoo-ids).

The sea pen has structures called polyps, which look like mini sea anemones. Each polyp has eight tentacles, making the sea pen belong to the 'octocorals' group.

Each polyp looks different and has a different job relating to its shape. Some form the central stalk, some bring in water and others are used for feeding.

A root-like structure, the 'peduncle' (ped-unk-ll) anchors the sea pen in sand or mud underwater, with the 'body' reaching up to 2m long. Although usually dull in colour, some sea pens are vivid orange. The sea pen is mostly anchored to the sea floor, but can move and anchor elsewhere to find more food, such as plankton, or to avoid predators.

It appears that, like trees, the sea pen has growth rings. If they are added each year, as they are in trees, then it seems that a sea pen can live for over 100 years.

It is said that long ago, people strongly believed that the tree held dragon's blood. The dragon's blood tree was very important in magic rituals and was used by alchemists to try to turn lead into gold.

DRAGON'S BLOOD TREE

ALIVE
~16 MYA–NOW
ASIA
AUTOTROPH

Many forms of life on Earth, whether animals, plants or fungi, have uses for humans, often as food or shelter. Some are said to have magical properties and have been important to us for hundreds or even thousands of years.

There are around 200 species of trees and succulent shrubs in the same group as the dragon's blood tree. Along with its relatives, the tree grows in an unusual way, called 'dracoid habitus', meaning 'the way of the dragon'. Its leaves are found only at the end of its youngest branches; everything underneath is bare branch. The old leaves are shed every three or four years. The tree's branches usually split either through flowering or the impact of herbivores trying to eat them.

The name comes from the blood red sap within the wood, which has, over time, had many uses, including medical properties.

There are tales about a rite of passage to prove bravery in which people place their hands into grass-woven gloves, with living ants stitched inside. The story goes that the ants sting so fiercely, it's one of the most painful experiences in the animal kingdom. The problem with this is that it's true.

Looking like stocky, red-black wingless wasps, the bullet ant measures 18–30mm long. Bullet ant colonies contain several hundred individuals and are usually found near the base of a tree. Worker ants climb the trunk to hunt for small invertebrate prey and to search for nectar, which they carry between their jaws back to the nest. All the members of the nest look similar, including the queen, which resembles the workers.

Despite its reputation, the bullet ant is not usually aggressive, unless a predator threatens. Before stinging, an angry bullet ant produces a warning sound by rubbing its legs against each other and against its body.

The bullet ant's sting currently ranks the highest of all insect stings, measured using a specially designed scale of pain. It is said to feel like 'walking over flaming charcoal with a nail embedded in your heel'. The pain is excruciating and can last for over 24 hours.

The '24 ant' or '24-hour ant', both alternative names for the bullet ant, refers to the full day of pain that follows being stung; it can also refer to the time it takes to kill a human.

BULLET ANT

- **ALIVE**
- **15+ MYA–NOW**
- **S AMERICA**
- **OMNIVORE**

NARWHAL

ALIVE
~500,000 YA–NOW
ARCTIC OCEAN
CARNIVORE

When the narwhal was first described, some people thought it used its long tusk to spear fish. The idea didn't really work because nobody could explain how, if that was the case, it could remove its catch afterwards.

So, what does the tusk in the males *actually* do? Maybe it's used to whack and stun fish, making them easier to catch. Most scientists agree it helps males display to female narwhals or scare off other males; perhaps both.

The tusk has millions of nerve endings that can pick up small changes in temperature, pressure and even the amount of salt in the seawater around a narwhal.

The narwhal eats a range of fish and squid, swimming up close to them and sucking them into its mouth. Although narwhals usually live in small groups, scientists have recorded over a thousand of them together.

Narwhals are incredible divers, reaching a depth of 2,370m, which makes them some of nature's deepest-diving whales.

FIDDLER CRAB

- ALIVE
- 20+ MYA–NOW
- WIDESPREAD BEACHES & COASTS
- DETRITIVORE

Competition in nature can take many forms, such as horns in sheep, coloured feathers in peacocks and even songs in gibbons, but fiddler crab males show off to each other by waving a massive claw. Only the male has the single very large claw. Female claws are the same size.

There are around a hundred species of fiddler crab, which all live partly on land, on beaches, mud flats, swamps and lagoons, not entirely underwater like many crabs. When not out displaying or feeding, the crabs live in burrows on a section of beach, where they might have several burrows.

Most are fairly small, with the biggest fiddler crab being 5cm across. Like all crabs, the fiddler sheds its external skeleton (its 'exoskeleton') as it grows. It is able to replace missing legs or claws, even the very large one, if lost through fighting or to predators.

A male has a range of signals, movements and meanings to its giant claw waving. These are intended to impress a female, who will choose her partner based on the size of his claw and the quality of the waving.

Sometimes when fiddler crab males fight, a big claw is lost. When this regrows, it's often weak and fragile, not strong enough for another fight. Other crabs don't know this though, so it's a bit of a sneaky way to con the other crabs, who don't realise the trick.

EURYPTERID

(yurr ip-terr-id)

EXTINCT
467.3–251.9 MYA
WIDESPREAD
PROBABLY CARNIVOROUS

It's easy to think prehistoric times were filled with giant dinosaurs, giant reptiles and giant mammals. But that's not completely accurate. There were giant invertebrates too and they would have been just as scary.

Eurypterid was the largest ever arthropod, the group of invertebrates with exoskeletons and jointed legs, which includes centipedes, crabs, spiders and trilobites. Some of the 250 or so species reached 2.5m in length, although many were much smaller, with the smallest measuring 2cm long.

All had six pairs of limbs, and differences in them help scientists separate eurypterids into two major groups. In one group, the sixth pair act as long, slender legs for walking. In the other group, these limbs are bigger and flattened to act as paddles for swimming. The rest of the legs in the 'paddling' group were quite small and probably only allowed them to crawl along the seabed when they weren't swimming. Other eurypterids had more powerful legs and were able to walk on land, like modern crabs.

So far, scientists haven't found any fossilised guts from a eurypterid, so we don't have strong evidence to show what they ate, but the rest of the body appears to suggest they were carnivores and hunted their prey.

The other name for the eurypterid is 'sea scorpion'. The difficulty here is that it was not a scorpion and only the earliest species lived in the sea. Others lived in fresh water.

MANCHINEEL TREE

ALIVE
~30 MYA–NOW
N, CENTRAL & S AMERICA
AUTOTROPH

It's raining so you shelter under a tree called the 'little apple', but you didn't read its full name: 'little apple of death'! It might already be too late for you, as you stand under the world's deadliest tree.

The manchineel tree grows up to 15m tall, has reddish-grey bark and small green-yellow flowers. Its shiny green leaves are up to 10cm long and are finely serrated or toothed.

After the tree flowers, it produces little green fruit that look like apples. These, and every other part of the tree, are highly poisonous. The milky-white sap, present in the tree's bark, leaves and fruit, contains different toxins that can cause severe blistering.

If you stand beneath the tree in the rain, sap can wash off and blister your skin so badly that you need to be rushed to hospital. If the wood is burned, the smoke can cause blindness.

If you confuse the fruit with an actual apple, you will initially taste something 'pleasant and sweet'. That changes to a 'strange peppery' taste, which develops into a burning sensation. Your throat will tighten and you'll experience terrible pain. The 'little apple of death' will have claimed its victim.

Where manchineels are found, it can be so unsafe to fell them that a red X or a red band is painted on the trunk or a fence is put up to stop you sheltering beneath it. In some places, a skull and crossbones sign tells you all you need to know.

APHID

♥ ALIVE
OVER 250 MYA–NOW
WORLDWIDE
HERBIVORE

Aphids are among the most common insects in the world – we've all seen them in the garden or park. They are incredible animals, with bizarre behaviours and fascinating reproduction.

The 5,000 or so species of aphid all have six long thin legs, which end in two little claws. Although most are wingless, winged forms are produced in many species at certain times of year. Most have a pair of tubes on the back of the abdomen that produce droplets of fast-hardening fluid to help defend against predators.

An aphid feeds using specialised mouthparts called a stylet which acts like a straw, piercing plants to reach the sap inside. The stylet sits inside a sheath made up from the jaws on the underside of its head. About ten per cent of aphid species are serious pests in gardens, farms and forests.

Some aphids have a fascinating relationship with certain ant species. These are called 'farming' or 'dairying' ants. They are like farmers and the aphids are like the cows. The aphid produces droplets of a sweet-tasting liquid called honeydew which the ants eat. In return, the ants protect the aphids from predators. The ants even 'milk' the aphids, by stroking their antennae, making them produce the honeydew.

An aphid is an unusual insect, because it gives birth to live young, rather than laying eggs. What's more, females can give birth to baby females who already have babies inside them, in a process called 'telescoping generations', all without the involvement of males.

TARANTULA WASP

- ALIVE
- 50 MYA–NOW
- WORLDWIDE
- ADULT: NECTARIVORE
  YOUNG: CARNIVORE

Described as 'quiet' and 'peaceful', this giant among wasps is a feared predator and is capable of delivering an unforgettably painful sting.

The tarantula wasp is any of the big wasps, measuring up to around 6.5cm, that hunt tarantulas. It's a name given to several groups, not a single specific species.

Among the largest wasps in the world, the tarantula wasp, also known as the tarantula hawk, usually has a blue-black body with orange-rust-coloured wings. This obvious and bright colouration is what scientists call an 'honest signal' and in this case, tells any possible predator this wasp can defend itself. Get too close and it'll sting, with a sizable stinger injecting potent venom.

The tarantula hawk is what is known as a 'parasitoid' (pa-ra sit-oyd) wasp, which means it acts as a parasite to other species. The female uses her sting to paralyse, but not kill, her prey. She then drags it into a brood nest to be 'living food'. One egg is laid on the prey, hatching into a larva, which eats the still-living host. So the victim stays alive for as long as possible, its internal organs are the last thing the developing larva eats.

The stinger of a female tarantula wasp can measure up to 12mm long. The powerful venom is recognised as one of the most painful insect stings in nature, second only to the bullet ant.

CONE SNAIL

- ♥ ALIVE
- ~40 MYA–NOW
- WIDESPREAD OCEANS
- CARNIVORE

Lots of us have picked up a shell from the water while on a trip to the beach. Now imagine the snail inside that pretty shell has a harpoon tipped with a venom so deadly it can kill an adult human. Would you still pick it up?

The 900 or so species of cone snails come in different sizes, patterns and colours, but, as you might guess, they are all shaped like cones, with one end like a round disc. The larger species of cone snails grow up to 23cm in length.

Every cone snail is venomous and can sting, using a specialised barbed 'tooth'. This can be shot out from the head of the snail at the end of a proboscis, which is a long flexible tube attached to the head of the snail and connected to the mouth. A venom gland delivers a powerful toxin, which paralyses the prey.

There is so much variation in the colours and patterns of these snails, that it's easy to confuse one for another, and although there are 900 or so species, there are over 3,000 different names for them. Would you be sure you knew whether you were holding a harmless or deadly snail?

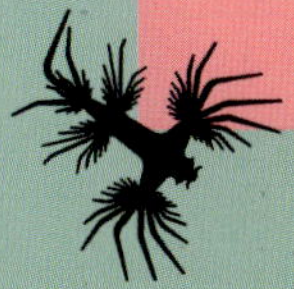

PIKAIA

(pik-ay-ur)

EXTINCT
513-505 MYA
N AMERICA
OMNIVORE (SORT OF)

It looked like a fish but wasn't, was once identified as a worm but wasn't, and appeared to have something like a skeleton that wasn't a skeleton. It might be one of the most important animals ever if you want to understand your own evolutionary family tree.

The body of the 3.5–5cm long *Pikaia* was flattened and narrowed at both ends. The head had two tentacles, like those on snails. The circular mouth had a row of small finger-like structures around it.

Fossils show that *Pikaia* had a notochord, which is a rod-like structure found in the embryos of vertebrates. In *Pikaia*, the flexible notochord would have run along the length of its back.

In vertebrates, the notochord usually disappears as the vertebrae and spinal cord develop in the growing embryo. But *Pikaia* didn't have a backbone or a spinal cord; it kept the notochord throughout its life.

Although *Pikaia* had structures to support it, like a skeleton, they were not made of bone. It's easy to think of *Pikaia* as an ancient fish, but without fins, scales or a complex skeletal framework, it wasn't. *Pikaia* was one of the earliest members of the group that would lead to vertebrates, making it incredibly important if we are to better understand our own group.

We can't say *Pikaia* is our direct ancestor. It's more accurate to say *Pikaia* was an ancient relative, living alongside animals which would eventually become vertebrates, from fish, amphibians, reptiles, birds and mammals and even you.

MANTIS SHRIMP

- ALIVE
- 359 MYA–NOW
- INDIAN & PACIFIC OCEANS
- CARNIVORE

Which animal would you least like to be punched by? A disgruntled gorilla? An impatient panda? What about by a small animal found on a coral reef, covered in splashes of colour, that can see things we can't imagine and with a punch so strong, it has a force similar to a bullet being fired from a gun?

There are over 520 species of mantis shrimp, meaning there are loads of differences in their size, colour, pattern and even in their famous limbs. Most are around 10cm long but some reach 38cm from head to tail. Some are camouflaged, while others are red, some are blue and stripy and others are all the colours of the rainbow.

The mantis shrimp has incredibly complex eyes and we don't properly understand yet how it sees the world. For a long time, we thought it could see colours we can't, but now we don't think that's quite right. It's more likely it can see different *types* of light, such as ultraviolet light, that we can't. It might also be sensitive to another type of light, which helps it see through the water more clearly and which, like a compass, may enable it to map where it is on a reef.

Different mantis shrimps have different types of limbs. Most are either smashers, which are used like clubs to punch their prey, or spearers, which have spines running along them.

ANTLION

- ALIVE
- 150 MYA–NOW
- WORLDWIDE
- CARNIVORE

There are many ways to catch food but if you're a larva lying at the bottom of a pit waiting until your victims fall in before dragging them under, it's a killer technique.

There are around 2,000 species of antlion. Adults all look a little like dragonflies, with two pairs of long, narrow wings and a long, slender abdomen. Wingspans are 2–15cm.

Unlike dragonflies, an antlion has long, club-tipped antennae. The larva has a fat, barrel-shaped body, with three pairs of legs. It has a flattened, square head with a massive pair of curved jaws, with hollow, sharp spines running down them. When the jaws fit together, they create a groove through which the larva injects venom. Its body is covered in forward-facing bristles, which anchor it in the sand to help pull in larger prey.

The antlion is found in dry, sandy habitats, where the larva can easily dig its pit. It piles little heaps of sand on its head, flicking grains up and outwards. The pit gradually gets deeper, until the angle of the slope becomes as steep as it can be, without sand collapsing into it. Buried at the centre of the pit, with only its jaws visible, the larva waits until unlucky prey slide down the pit walls.

Unusually, the antlion larva does not have a bum. Any waste produced is stored, with some of it being used to make silk for a cocoon, when the antlion changes from larva to adult.

GOBI JERBOA

ALIVE
~5 MYA–NOW
ASIA
OMNIVORE

It's easy to think of kangaroos as the kings and queens of bouncing behaviour. But a group of small, desert-living rodents are also excellent hoppers and bouncers.

The Gobi jerboa looks a little like a miniature kangaroo, with some physical similarities. Both have long hind legs, short forelegs and long tails. Both hop well, but that's where the similarities end. A kangaroo can bounce repeatedly for long distances and for hours at a time. A Gobi jerboa is better suited to short bursts of movement, with lots of twists and turns, and it can perform massive leaps when it needs to escape a predator. Living in deserts and grasslands, it faces a lot of potential predators, so it needs to be able to get away. When chased, it can run as speedily as 24 km/h, faster than a human sprinting.

Its ears are its most obvious feature, because they are so large. Nearly three times as large as its head, they allow the Gobi jerboa to have a very good sense of hearing and help to cool its body in the intense heat of the desert.

The Gobi jerboa is a nocturnal rodent, which lives alone and spends most of the daytime in a tunnel, up to 60cm beneath the ground. It has little chambers within this tunnel, for sleeping.

If it does not feel threatened, the Gobi jerboa will make little hops of about 10–13cm, but if there's a predator close by, it can jump up to 3m.

AXOLOTL

(ack-sur lot-ol)

ALIVE
157 MYA–NOW
MEXICO
CARNIVORE

The axolotl has attracted the attention of scientists for its remarkable ability to heal and regenerate body parts. It does not scar as we do, but can regrow toes, entire limbs, its tail and even parts of its eyes and brain.

If you cut your finger, it will heal in a few days. If you cut your finger *off*, then you need to get to hospital quickly. But for one salamander, such an injury is no problem. It'll just regrow.

Unlike most amphibians, young and adult axolotl look similar and do not undergo a major transformation, like tadpoles into frogs. Unusually, the axolotl continues to grow larger throughout its life, while still looking like a juvenile.

The adult axolotl can measure 15–45cm long, although it's rare to see one longer than 30cm. The adult axolotl has a fin stretching from head to tail and external, branch-like gills behind its head. The gills move water over them, increasing the flow. This enables more oxygen to be passed through the gill tissue, so the axolotl can draw in more oxygen.

This predatory amphibian mainly lives alone, waiting for food to get within reach.

Detecting a possible meal through smell, the axolotl creates a suction force by folding its gills back over its gill slits when small fish, worms, snails or other invertebrates get close. Although the axolotl is a common pet, there may be as few as 100 left in the wild.

VELVET WORM

ALIVE
300+ MYA–NOW
WIDESPREAD
CARNIVORE

Known also as '*Peripatus*', this many-legged animal has been compared to a 'turbo-caterpillar' and a worm with legs. With at least 200 species, the velvet worm is a small, yet fearsome, predator.

Depending on the species, a velvet worm can measure 0.1–22cm. The number of legs can vary from 13 pairs to as many as 43. The body has a series of fine rings running down it, and ranges in colour from orange, red or brown, to white, blue, green or gold.

On either side of the mouth are two little openings. Inside these are large, complex slime glands. A slime conductor is connected to the slime gland allowing the velvet worm to store pre-produced slime. The slime is released through a syringe-like system, where muscles are squeezed, forcing the slime out at incredibly high speeds of up to 5m per second. The slime both distracts predators and traps prey, shooting up to 30cm.

The velvet worm's movement is so slow it often goes undetected until it is literally able to touch its victim. Using its antennae to assess whether the prey is a good size and edible, the velvet worm then squirts slime over its target. It then, very slowly, chases the prey until it is no longer able to run, as it is immobilised in the sticky slime.

The velvet worm can target specific parts of the body with its slime. If it encounters a spider, it will spray slime directly on to the dangerous biting mouthparts.

FIREFLY

- ALIVE
- 99 MYA–NOW
- WORLDWIDE
- SOME SPECIES CARNIVORES, SOME HERBIVORES

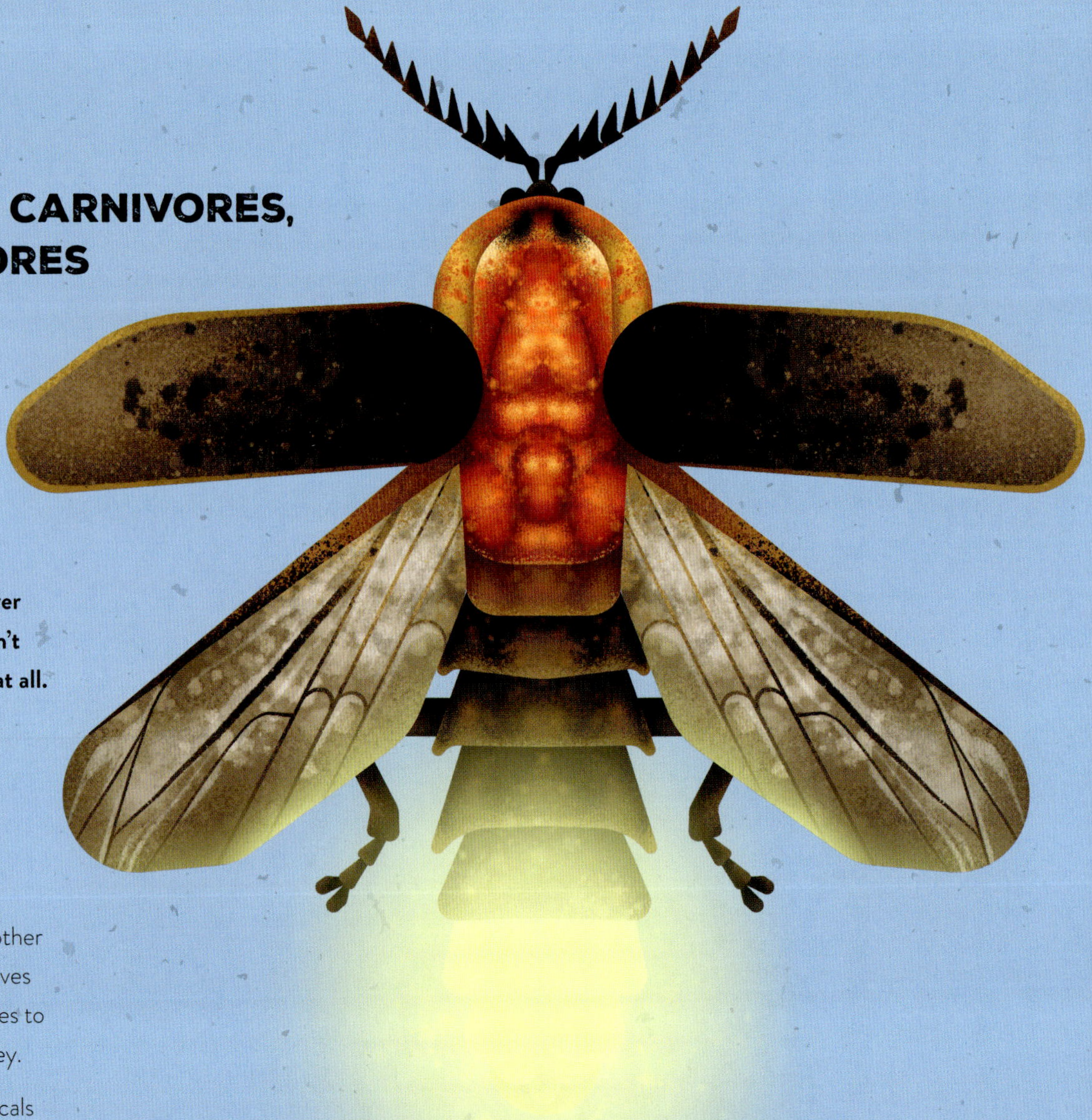

Fireflies are found across the planet and are also known as glow-worms or lightning bugs. There are over 2,000 species of firefly and they aren't actually worms or bugs or even flies, at all. They are light-producing beetles.

Fireflies vary in colour and shape and although some are small, the biggest are up to 2.5cm long. The larvae of many species are specialist predators and eat slugs, snails and the larvae of other insects. Some larvae have special grooves running along their teeth-like mandibles to deliver digestive juices straight into prey.

A firefly creates light by mixing chemicals inside its body. When the chemicals mix, they react and produce light. The firefly produces this light to attract a mate. In many species, large numbers gather and all flash together, pulsing their light organs. In some tropical zones, especially along riverbanks, entire clouds flash away together, like a natural forest light party.

The female in some of the larger species flashes its light in exactly the same way as smaller species. When the small male comes looking for a mate, it is often eaten by the larger female predator.

EUROPEAN EEL

ALIVE
80-40 MYA–NOW
EUROPE, AFRICA & SARGASSO SEA
CARNIVORE

European eels usually live 15–20 years in the wild, but a family in Sweden claimed an eel had lived in their well for 155 years.

The European eel's life history was a mystery for centuries, as nothing identified as a young eel was ever caught. The reality behind these global migrators is extraordinary.

This fish has a long, snake-like body. An adult measures 100–130cm long and can twist and turn, thanks to 110–120 vertebrae running through its body. It feeds mainly at night, using its keen sense of smell to hunt worms, slugs, crabs, crayfish and fish.

Wherever a European eel lives, it must swim to a small area of the western Atlantic Ocean, called the Sargasso Sea, to spawn. The young will return here when it is their time to reproduce.

The eel has very different life stages. Hatching in the Sargasso Sea, a leaf-shaped larva joins the warm waters that transport it across the Atlantic. In the second stage, the larva turns into a 'glass eel' at some point in its ocean journey, which might take a year or two. When it reaches shore, it turns into a finger-length, transparent 'glass eel'.

The 'elver' is the third stage, when the young eel darkens and moves into a freshwater habitat. Fourth stage, the 'yellow eel' is the early adult phase. Its belly becomes yellow. In the fifth and final stage, the 'silver eel' is ready to reproduce and it starts the long journey back to the Sargasso Sea.

GREATER FRIGATE BIRD

- ALIVE
- 1.5 MYA–NOW
- TROPICAL SEAS
- CARNIVORE

We've all heard stories of pirates causing mayhem on the seven seas, but in nature there is a real pirate, with a reputation for theft and chaos.

Reaching over 1m in length, this great black seabird has a green-purple sheen to its feathers, with a white throat streak. In the breeding season, the male inflates a huge red throat sac. Its wingspan may be as much as 2.3m, about the length of two six-year-old humans lying head to toe. It has the lowest wing loading of any bird.

Wing loading is the weight supported by the area of the wings and helps us understand efficiency in flying. A low wing loading allows a bird to maximise its lift and fly like a glider aeroplane, allowing it to twist and turn as it chases other birds.

The greater frigate bird hunts on the wing by snatching prey from just below the surface (such as squid) or from the air (flying fish). Like other frigate birds, it may not be able to take off again if it lands on water. It also steals food by chasing other birds and making them throw up their food. In one study, up to 40 per cent of the greater frigate's food was gained from this sort of piracy.

If you held all this bird's feathers in one hand and all its bones in another, it is said the feathers would weigh more than the bones, meaning the greater frigate bird is a really lightweight aerial predator.

BABIRUSA

(bab-ir ruu-sa)

ALIVE
26-12 MYA-NOW
INDONESIA
OMNIVORE

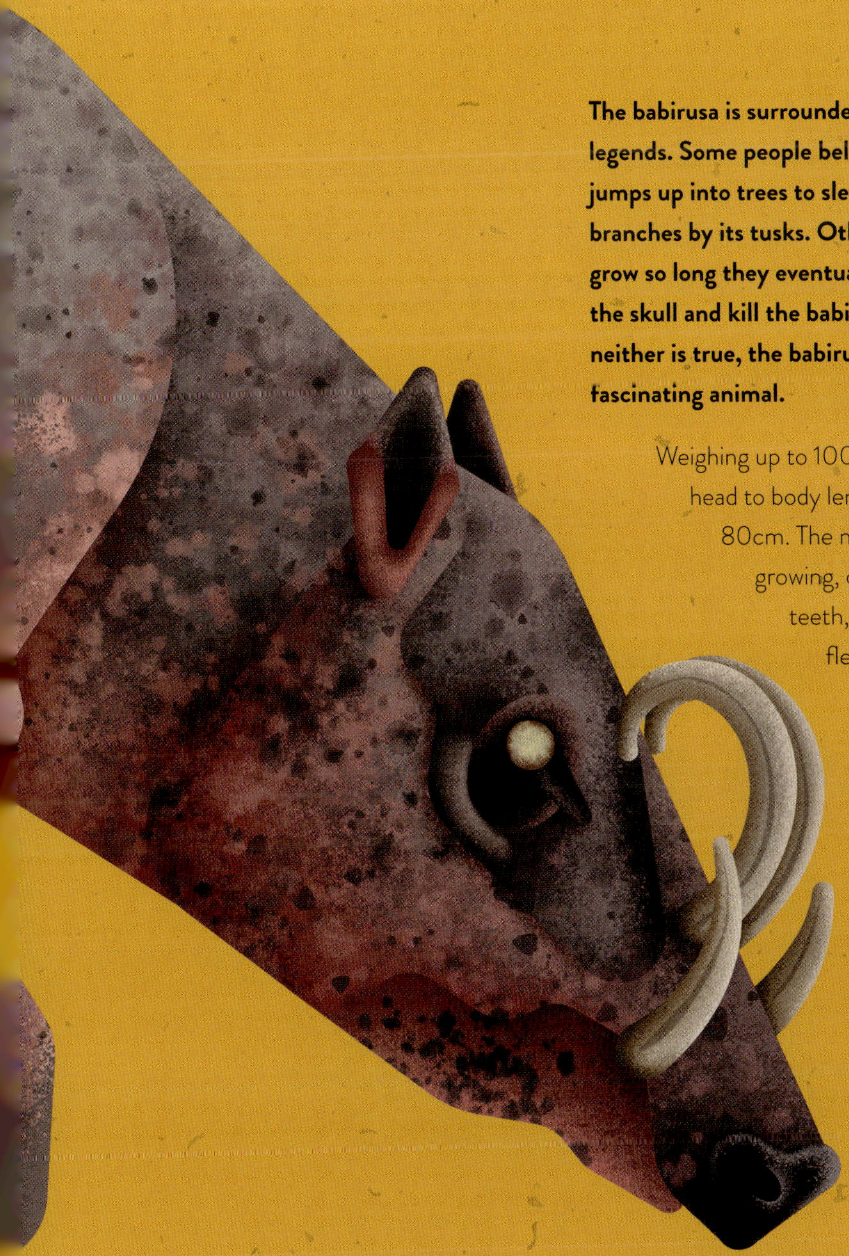

The babirusa is surrounded by myth and legends. Some people believe the babirusa jumps up into trees to sleep, hanging from branches by its tusks. Others say the tusks grow so long they eventually push into the skull and kill the babirusa. Although neither is true, the babirusa remains a fascinating animal.

Weighing up to 100kg, the babirusa's head to body length is up to 80cm. The male has upward-growing, curved canine teeth, which pierce the flesh in its snout.

These tusks can reach 40cm long and grow throughout the animal's life. The canines in the female are either much smaller or sometimes not present at all.

The babirusa prefers to live in tropical rainforests along riverbanks. It is also found on higher ground and away from the coast, but this is most likely to avoid human settlements.

The babirusa is active during the day and, like all members of the pig family, it is an omnivore and eats leaves, fruits, roots and even small animals. It does not have a bony nose plate like many other pigs though, so does not forage or dig with its nose.

Scientists believe the babirusa might be the oldest living member of the pig family. There are 35,000-year-old cave paintings showing the babirusa with its distinctive tusks, and its monster-like appearance inspired some scary traditional ceremony masks in Indonesia.

TASSELED WOBBEGONG

ALIVE
2 MYA–NOW
AUSTRALASIA
CARNIVORE

Scientists spotted a tasselled wobbegong eating a bamboo shark that was 80 per cent the wobbegong's size.

How long will you wait for something, before you get bored? A few minutes? What about days, without so much as a twitch of your little finger? There is one reef-dwelling predator who can play the ultimate game of patience.

The tasselled wobbegong is a type of carpet shark, which looks a lot flatter than most sharks you'd imagine. Reaching around 1.8m in length, it has a head that is wider than it is long. Around its head sits a 'frill' of flaps, projections and tassels, which breaks up the outline of the head against the sandy seabed, camouflaging the wobbegong in its surroundings. Its body is covered in spots, blotches and other markings to further help conceal it.

Inside its mouth are up to 26 rows of teeth in the upper jaw and 19 rows in the lower jaw. In the middle of each of these are three rows (in the upper jaw) and two rows (in the bottom jaw), where the teeth are especially long and fang-like.

The tasselled wobbegong is an expert at sitting and waiting, like the perfect ambush hunter. As soon as something like a fish gets within range, the wobbegong strikes and opens its huge mouth wide. This sudden opening of the mouth creates a difference in the water pressure, causing the fish to be sucked into the wobbegong's waiting jaws.

MILKWEED ASSASSIN BUG

ALIVE
70 MYA–NOW
N, CENTRAL & S AMERICA
CARNIVORE

Some assassin bugs use natural resins from plants such as certain grasses to help them catch a meal. Rubbing the sticky glue on their hairy legs helps the bugs trap prey more successfully.

If you were a small insect, looking for tasty plants to eat, there is one garden inhabitant you would want to avoid. If you were unlucky enough to be caught by this predator it would dissolve your organs and suck out the juices like a meaty milkshake.

The milkweed assassin bug is a combination of bright orange and black and measures 14–20mm long. It has a long, thin head, a narrow neck and spindly legs. Its mouthparts look like a pointed dart, which it tucks beneath its head and rests on the underside of its body in a special groove. These mouthparts are known as the 'rostrum'.

The bug moves its rostrum within the groove, producing a vibrating sound to scare off predators. If that doesn't work, the bug can then use its sharp rostrum to stab would-be attackers.

The milkweed assassin bug's rostrum is most often used for feeding. It stabs its prey with the tip and injects it with a deadly saliva (spit). This contains chemicals called enzymes, which digest organs and tissue. Once the victim's insides have dissolved, the predator sucks up the meal.

SPARKLEMUFFIN

- ALIVE
- NO FOSSILS SO FAR
- AUSTRALIA
- CARNIVORE

When we think of spiders, it's often those big, scuttling brown ones. But some are brightly coloured, able to leap huge distances and have funny-sounding names.

A sparklemuffin is big on style but small in size. Males are around 4mm long but females are a little bigger, up to 6mm, meaning even the biggest sparklemuffin is only the size of a grain of rice. The sparklemuffin belongs to a group called the peacock spiders. Male peacock spiders are brightly coloured, while females are usually brown or black. The flashy male sparklemuffin has grey legs and an abdomen patterned with bright red and blue stripes. Some scientists think sparklemuffins have such incredible vision that they may be able to see as well as cats.

The male sparklemuffin doesn't dance because it loves music, but to impress a mate so it can breed. When the male is a few centimetres away from the female, he raises a pair of legs and starts waving them around. He then unwraps little flaps on his abdomen and waves them around too. If things work and the female is interested, he vibrates as she gets closer. Sometimes, though, the female is simply not impressed and bad dancers get eaten.

A sparklemuffin can jump 50 times the length of its own body. This is impressive, especially when you realise it's like an average ten-year-old human leaping the length of almost seven double-decker buses.

CARNUFEX

(car-nu feks)

- EXTINCT
- 231 MYA
- N AMERICA
- CARNIVORE

For most of us, the thought of encountering a hungry crocodile or alligator is pretty scary, but the ones alive today don't sound quite as frightening when you discover there was once a large, two-legged ancient crocodile relative that could probably run faster than you.

Carnufex is an early member of the modern crocodilian lineage, and was very different to members of this group alive today. It did not live in the water and it walked on two legs, not four, most likely hunting by stalking on two legs, then chasing prey over short bursts.

Carnufex would have been about 3m long and at least 1.5m tall. Some of the body proportions are a little unexpected in *Carnufex*, with a bigger skull and shorter arms than modern crocodiles. The skull was heavily textured and almost looked as if it had decorations with ridges, lumps and bumps. This may have been for display to other, male or female, *Carnufex*.

Because the fossils from *Carnufex* are so old, it pushes the timeline for crocodile ancestors to a much older point than we previously imagined. From the fossils found so far, it is likely *Carnufex* was the largest predator in its environment.

The name *Carnufex* means 'butcher', which definitely doesn't help the reputation of this fearsome prehistoric relative of the crocodile.

VOLCANO SNAIL

ALIVE
30+ MYA–NOW
INDIAN OCEAN
DOESN'T EAT

Compared to other snails, the volcano snail has a big heart. This allows it to keep both the bacteria and itself alive in the deep sea, where there is little oxygen.

The deepest parts of the Earth's oceans are dark, hostile places. The pressure is crushing, with scalding, poisonous, highly acidic natural chimneys, or hydrothermal vents, called 'black smokers'. To survive here, any animal needs amazing defences.

The volcano snail has a unique shell made from three layers, each section acting differently. The outer layer is the thinnest but toughest. It's made from particles of hard material called iron sulphide ('fool's gold'), which the snail obtains from the black smokers. It will blunt a crab's claws if one tries to attack, and any cracks made by a crab will be tiny and actually help act as shock absorbers.

The middle layer is soft and spongy, absorbing crab attacks. The boundary between this and the outer layer appears wavy, meaning they 'stick' together better and are stronger.

The third layer, like the shell of most snails, is made from calcium carbonate. If the shell was made only from this substance, it would dissolve in the acidic waters around the vents, leaving the snail homeless.

The volcano snail doesn't actually *need* to eat. It has a special relationship with bacteria inside its gut. The bacteria live safely there and the snail benefits from the bacteria releasing energy directly to it.

FIRE CORAL

ALIVE
265+ MYA–NOW
WIDESPREAD OCEANS
CARNIVORE

Although it may sound like a type of coral and look like a coral, fire corals are more closely related to jellyfish. The 'fire' part of the name is more accurate, because the last thing you want to do is touch one.

Most fire coral is orange or yellow, but it can be brown, green or blue. There is a lot of variation in size and shape across the different species. Some grow in sheets, spreading like a flat coat over rocks. Others look more like trees, with stems and branches. The ends of these branches are rounded, finger-shaped tips and are often white.

It's hard to look at this tree-like structure and think it's an animal, but it's more complicated than that. The fire coral is what is known as a 'colonial organism' made up of many smaller organisms, working together. It has long, fine hair-like structures with specialist cells that are capable of delivering a painful sting. It uses these to defend itself or to capture prey, pulling it into specialist feeding chambers called polyps.

Fire coral is found in shallow reefs where it can catch the most sunlight, so algae living inside the structure can photosynthesise and produce more energy. Fire coral appears to thrive where there is a high, strong current and warm water.

If you are unlucky enough to brush against a fire coral and it stings you, you'll feel intense fiery pain for up to two weeks, so best to avoid them on a swim.

TULLY MONSTER

EXTINCT
311–306 MYA
FOSSILS FOUND IN N AMERICA
CARNIVORE

In a famous film about a galactic superhero, there's a line, 'Is it a bird? Is it a plane?' Luckily, in science, we're rarely confused about what something is, but sometimes, something confusing comes along.

The Tully monster could grow to 35cm long, but most fossils are around 8cm. It had a torpedo-shaped body, narrowed at either end, and two vertical, triangular fins at its tail end.

At its head was a proboscis, a little like the arm of a crane. The end opened into a mouth, with up to eight small, sharp teeth in each jaw. Behind this sat a little stalk branching out from either side of the body. At the end of this structure were its eyes. This was an animal unlike anything alive today, but what was it?

It appears the Tully monster was a free-swimming marine carnivore, living and hunting in open water. Some scientists believe it was a very, very old member of the vertebrate family, leading to all animals with a spinal cord and a series of backbones. Others say it was a type of ancient invertebrate, or perhaps an invertebrate with a spine-like structure, but neither one nor the other.

Scientists have suggested the Tully monster was an ancient member of the snail and slug family, or the crab and lobster group, or a type of worm, a sea squirt, an ancient jawless vertebrate, or a strange member of the fish family. The truth is, we still don't know.

OCEAN SUNFISH

ALIVE
50,000 YA–NOW
WIDESPREAD OCEANS
CARNIVORE

Imagine growing to 60 million times bigger than when you were born. That's exactly what happens with adult ocean sunfish, after they hatch at just 2.5mm long. This huge growth spurt might be the most extreme of any vertebrate animal on the planet.

Although not quite the heaviest bony fish in the world, it's definitely within the top three, reaching a weight of up to a tonne, about the same as a camel. Its cousin, the giant sunfish, is a little heavier and claims the record. The sunfish looks as though someone has taken a really big fish head and stuck a tail on it, forgotting to add the body. It looks flattened and can be as tall as it is long when the fins on the top (dorsal) and bottom (ventral) of its body are extended. Some ocean sunfish are over 3m in height.

As with so many animals, we find out about these the more we study them. For a long time, scientists thought sunfish only ate jellyfish, but by using special tests that reveal the DNA of food in sunfish stomachs, we now know they eat a range of fish, squid, crabs and some plants too. Jellyfish make up about 15 per cent of their diet, leaving 85 per cent for other types of food.

Baby sunfish look like mini pufferfish, to which they're closely related. They swim in spiky little groups for protection, but move more on their own as they grow older.

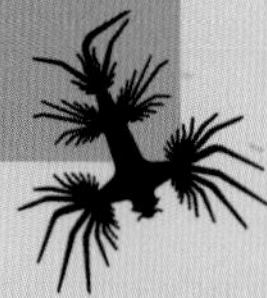

GOBLIN SHARK

- ALIVE
- 49–37 MYA–NOW
- WIDESPREAD OCEANS
- CARNIVORE

Sharks come in all shapes and sizes as there are hundreds of species, but the deep-sea, bright pink goblin shark is truly one of a kind.

Usually growing to 3–4m long but able to reach up to 6m, it is a significant predator. Its long, blade-like snout is able to sense weak electrical currents produced by other animals, but it is probably not used to stir up the seabed to search for hidden prey. Below the snout, in its mouth are hundreds of curved, thin nail-like teeth, sitting in rows. The top jaw has 35–53 tooth rows and the lower jaw has 31–62. The pink (or sometimes tan) colour is due to the visible blood vessels beneath its skin. The colour deepens as the shark gets older. Baby goblin sharks may be almost white.

The goblin shark eats fish, squid, octopus, crabs and their relatives, hunting on the seabed and higher up in the water column. When it senses prey, it slings its mouth forward, almost as far as the tip of the snout.

Although it is a large and powerful hunter, the goblin shark appears to be a slow and sluggish swimmer. Its skeleton seems to be weaker than that of many other sharks and even its fins are small.

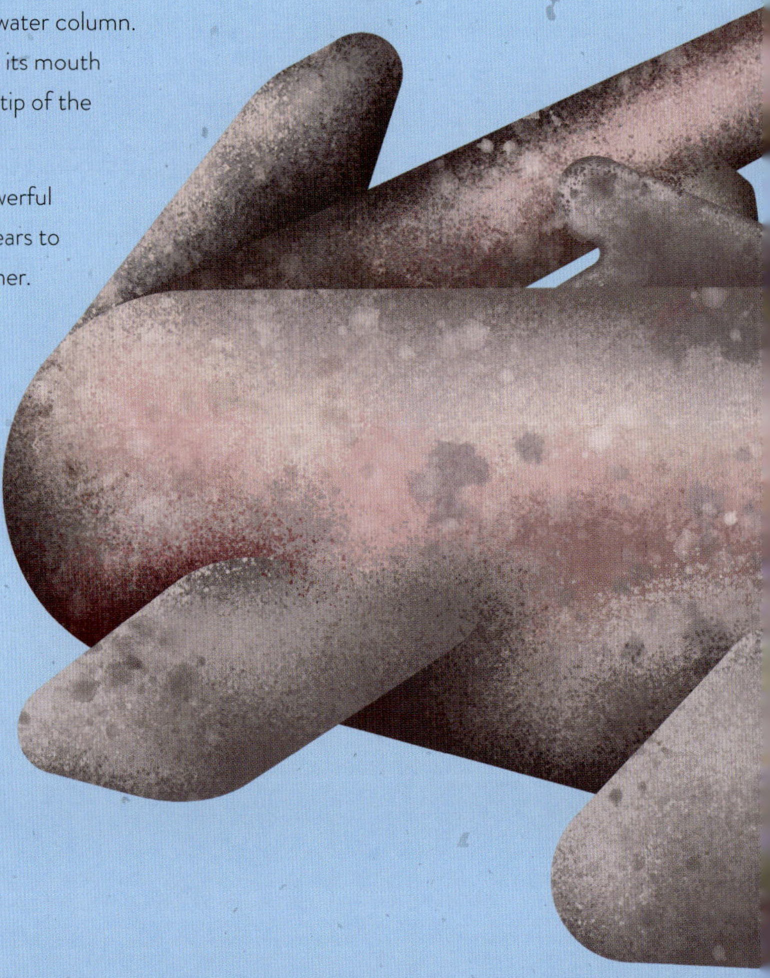

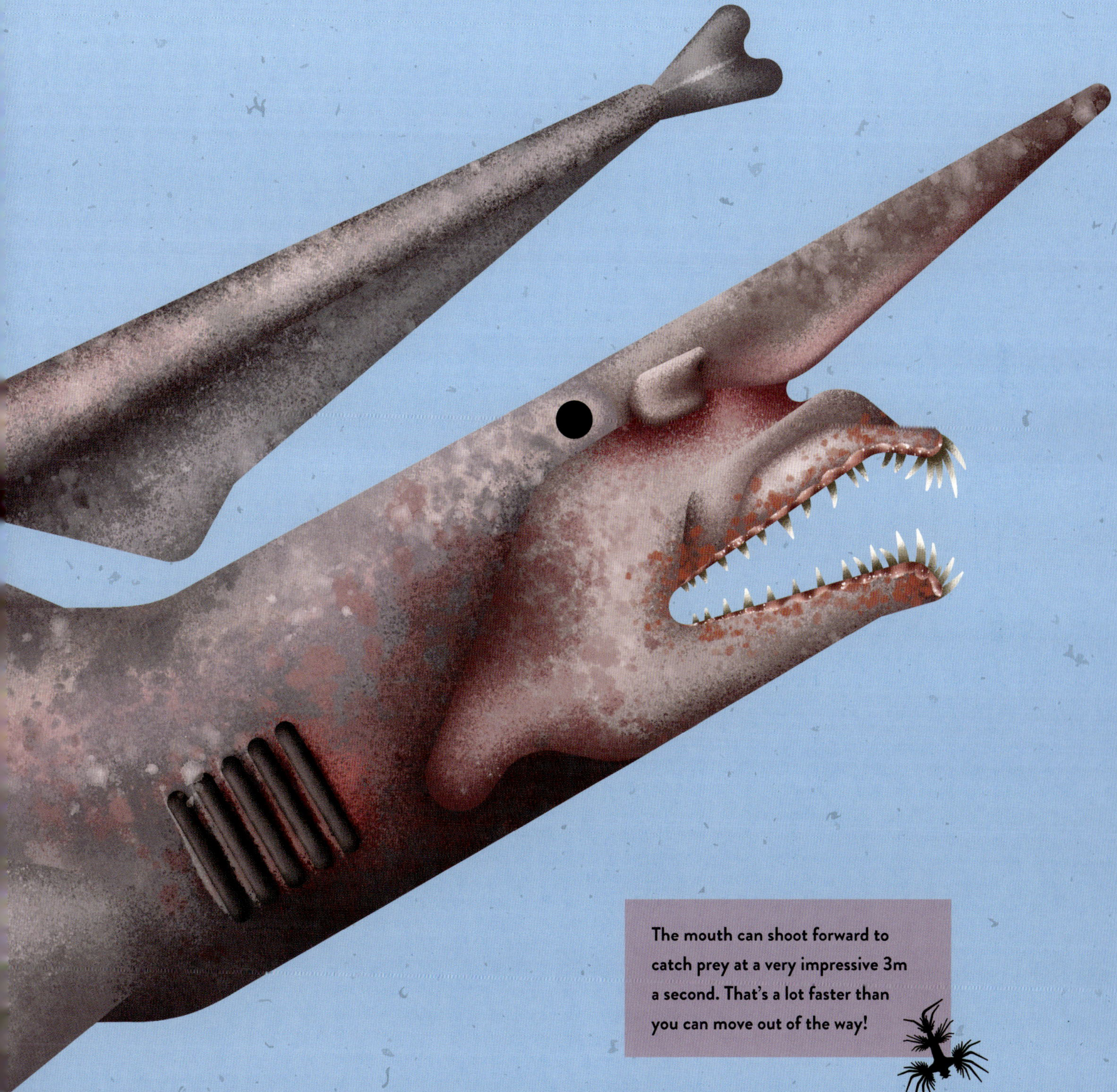

The mouth can shoot forward to catch prey at a very impressive 3m a second. That's a lot faster than you can move out of the way!

THYLACOSMILUS

(thyl-akko smile-us)

EXTINCT
9-3 MYA
S AMERICA
CARNIVORE

We know a lot about sabre-toothed cats, but there is a famous prehistoric sabre-toothed marsupial that was just as deadly. Except it wasn't technically a marsupial, and may not even have been a predator! *Thylacosmilus* is a good example of why we should never judge a book by its cover.

Looking similar to the enormous sabre-toothed cats such as *Smilodon*, *Thylacosmilus* was always said to be the 'marsupial sabre-tooth'. It was once considered to be a true marsupial, but we now know *Thylacosmilus* belonged to a separate group of animals, closely related to the kangaroos, wallabies, wombats and other marsupials we see today. It weighed 80–150kg, close to the size and weight of a jaguar. Its massive teeth continued to grow throughout the animal's life. More than half of each canine was embedded in special channels in the skull, to anchor them.

Although *Thylacosmilus* had massive killing teeth, scientific evidence tells a different story. There were no sharp incisor teeth to strip and tear meat, the bite force was fairly weak, and the two halves of the lower jaw were not fully fused in the middle. The large teeth themselves were also the wrong shape for slashing and stabbing. Instead, it's likely *Thylacosmilus* was a specialist scavenger and may have used its canines to tear open bodies to feed on the softer organs inside.

So much about *Thylacosmilus* seems to be a case of mistaken identity – even its name means 'cruel pouch-knife'.

GABOON VIPER

- ALIVE
- ~5 MYA-NOW
- AFRICA
- CARNIVORE

There's a snake with bigger fangs and more venom than any other snake. It is one of the most toxic animals on the planet, but has a reputation for being pretty chilled out and even friendly. This is the gaboon viper.

Usually around 155cm in length, this is a solid, heavy-looking snake. The circumference of its body can be 37cm, which is huge for a snake of this size. It can weigh up to 8.5kg, which adds to the idea of a stocky powerful snake. There is a report of a female (without eggs and with an empty stomach) weighing a massive 11.3kg. The large head is triangular and a pair of 'horns' sits between raised nostrils. Its fangs can reach 5.5cm in length.

Unusually for a snake, this viper mostly moves in a straight line. By moving its tummy scales against each other, it appears to 'walk'.

A slow-moving, nocturnal snake, it hunts by waiting, often completely motionless, for long periods, before ambushing its prey and striking. Unlike most vipers, it is said to be non-aggressive. But there's no way you should get close enough to find out if that's true, as this is one of the fastest-striking snakes in the world. When it does strike, it doesn't let go either. It just pumps in that massive dose of deadly venom.

Gaboon vipers eat anything, from doves and guinea fowl to frogs and lizards. They will even take monkeys, porcupines and small antelope.

TARDIGRADE

(tar-dee grayd)

ALIVE
90+ MYA (MAYBE AS MUCH AS 500 MYA)–NOW
WORLDWIDE
OMNIVORE

If you could design an animal that was able to survive in extreme cold and heat, very high and very low pressures, radiation and even starvation, what would this amazing beast look like? Would you be surprised to know it's already living in your local park, your school playing field and probably your back garden?

There are over 1,000 species of tardigrades, all eight-legged, segmented, 'micro-animals'. Short and plump, they have four pairs of unjointed legs, each ending in sticky pads or claws. Tardigrades range in length from 0.1 to 0.5mm, although the largest species may reach 1.3mm.

A tardigrade does not have lungs, gills or blood vessels. It transfers air back and forth between the waxy shell-like covering and body cavity to obtain oxygen and remove carbon dioxide.

It is found on land and in the oceans, from shallow water to deep sea depths. It lives in tropical rainforests, high on mountain tops and in cities. It is often found living in and around mosses and lichens and is able to survive in most places, from very warm climates to incredibly cold habitats, even in Antarctica. Tardigrades were taken to outer space to see what effect that had. No problem, they survived that too.

A tardigrade may have the best survival attributes of any animal on the planet but it is also known as a 'water bear' or 'moss piglet', which sounds more cute than impressive.

ZOMBIE WORM

- ALIVE
- 100 MYA–NOW
- WORLDWIDE OCEANS
- OSSIVORE

Do you have any strange eating habits? There is one deep-sea diner with a very unusual approach to mealtimes. The zombie worm, known also as the 'bone worm', feeds on the skeletons of dead whales, even though it doesn't even have a mouth!

This is nothing like the worms in your garden. As well as no mouth, the zombie worm has no stomach and no bum. Its feathery-looking gills take oxygen from the water. It looks like a tiny plant, with a section known as the 'trunk' and an area of 'roots', which help it attach to the surface of a whale bone. Then it uses strong, slimy acid and 'friendly' bacteria to feed. The worm releases the acid through its skin, dissolving the bone and creating a little tunnel to get to the fats stored in it. Special bacteria living in and on the zombie worm's body digest these fats, but how the worm itself gets these fats from the bacteria is still a puzzle.

Some male zombie worms are only 0.4mm long, but females can be 100,000 times larger. Being so much smaller means males don't compete for food. It also means they can actually live inside the female's body. Some females can house over 100 miniature males. An 'ovisac' in female zombie worms stores the eggs.

One species of zombie worm has a scientific name which means 'bone-eating snot flower'.

SAWFISH

- ALIVE
- 60 MYA–NOW
- WORLDWIDE OCEANS
- CARNIVORE

There is a group of five living species of a ray that are so enormous, so unusual and so ancient they look as if they could have fought dinosaurs.

Sawfish are usually a dull shade of grey, brown, yellow or green, although some are almost black. The underside is pale, or completely white. They are among the largest fish on the planet and can reach more than 7.5m long, although such giants are rare nowadays.

The sawfish gets its name from its most obvious feature, its saw-like snout, called a rostrum. This is a long projection of its skull above the mouth, with what looks like big, sharp teeth running the length on either side and around the tip. These 'teeth' are actually special scales, adapted from the rough-edged scales (or denticles) we see on sharks and rays. The rostrum is around a quarter of the total length of the sawfish and has 28–74 'teeth'. There are 170–300 actual teeth in its mouth.

Sawfish feed on fish and invertebrates, detected and captured with their saw. The underside of the rostrum has lots of little pits which sense tiny electrical impulses released by prey in the mud or sand.

It appears that ancient species of sawfish lived alongside dinosaurs. The fossilised 'teeth' of huge sawfish have been found embedded in the skulls of the famous fishing dinosaur, *Spinosaurus*.

MIDWIFE TOAD

- ALIVE
- 8 MYA–NOW
- EUROPE, AFRICA
- CARNIVORE

Some animals really take care of their developing young, keeping them safe in a nest or hiding them from danger. One little amphibian carries its eggs on its back until they are ready to hatch.

The midwife toad is fairly small, growing to around 5cm in length, about as long as your little finger. There are five species, all small and plump with warty skin, which is mostly dull grey, green or brown. The female toad sometimes has red spots on her sides.

The midwife toad is best known for the way it looks after its young. Once the female has released a strand of eggs, the male wraps them around his legs to protect them from predators in the water. After around six weeks of development, the male finds some shallow water, which will be safe from predators. He dunks the eggs in the water, allowing the tadpoles to hatch and begin their own journey.

Although small, the midwife makes a loud call to attract a mate. Males and females create a high-pitched whistle, which some people say reminds them of the sound a smoke detector makes when its battery is running low.

The name 'midwife toad' is confusing on many levels. It's the male, not the female, who is responsible for the care of the eggs, so 'midwife' may need a rethink; and the midwife toad is actually a frog too.

SILVERFISH

- ALIVE
- 400 MYA–NOW
- WIDESPREAD
- OMNIVORE

You may have seen a flash of silver at the back of the garden shed when you open the door, or something glittering as it scurries away in your granny's bathroom as you reach for a towel, and you probably didn't give it a second thought. But you'll have just met one of the oldest and most successful animals on the planet.

The silverfish is a 13–25mm long, wingless, nocturnal insect. Its name comes from its silvery light-grey colour, combined with its fish-like wiggling movement. Its head is rounded but its abdomen becomes thinner and thinner and quite narrow at the tail end. It has three long strands at the tip of its abdomen, with the central one being the longest. It has a small pair of eyes and long antennae.

The silverfish is rarely welcome in a home, because of its ability to eat things! It mainly feeds on sugars and starches. You might think sugar comes mostly from sweets and starch from potatoes, but your home is actually one big buffet for silverfish. They eat books (but hopefully not this one), clothing, coffee, carpets, glue, paper, paints, building plaster, wallpaper paste, cotton, leather, dead insects, crumbs of food, human hair and even dandruff.

Silverfish can live for up to three years but are actually able to go a whole year without eating, as long as water is available.

MEGALODON

- EXTINCT
- 23–2.6 MYA
- WIDESPREAD OCEANS
- CARNIVORE

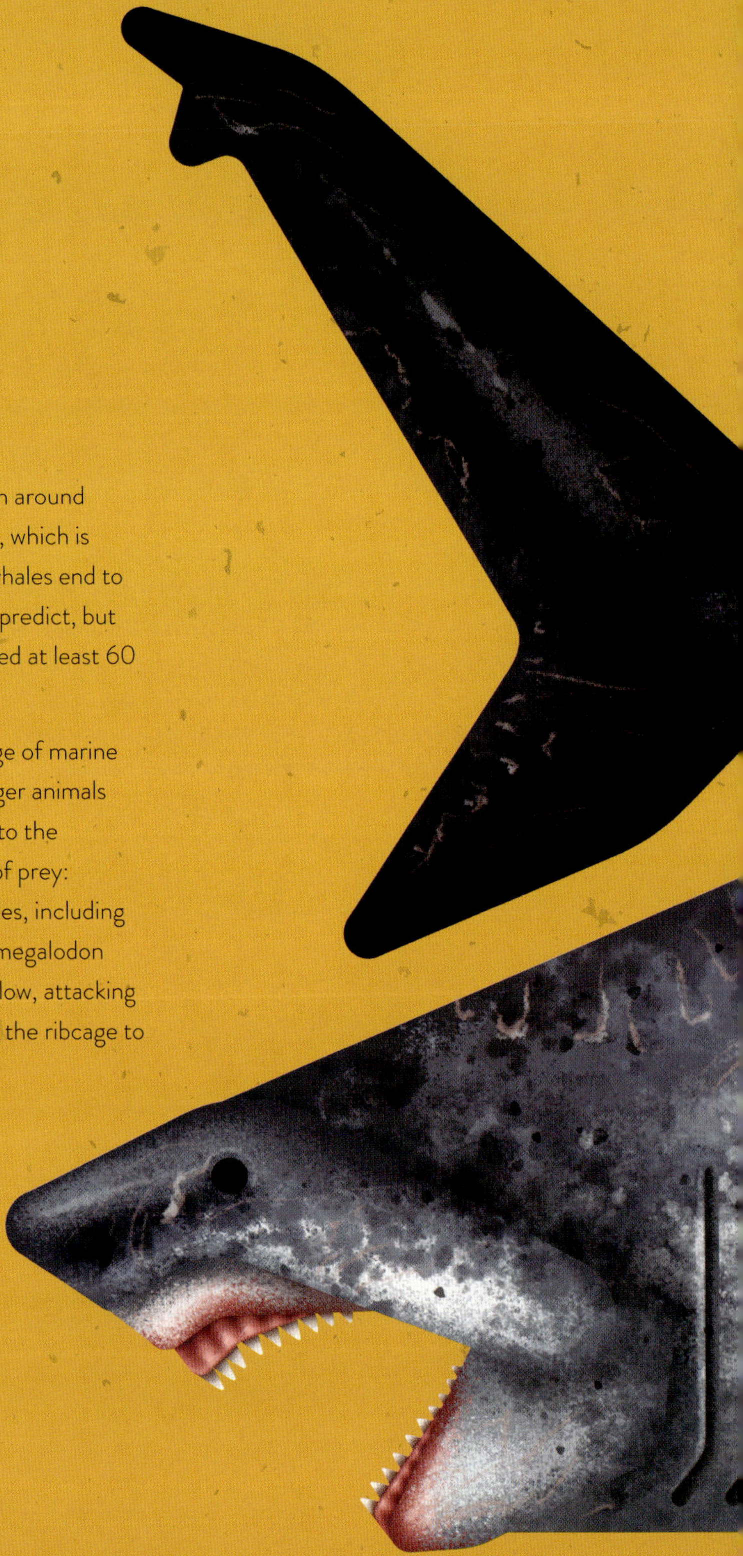

Sometimes, fact *is* scarier than fiction. There have been many fearsome sharks in films and books over the years, but however immense, mean and scary they look, there has only ever been one ultimate marine predator: megalodon.

Although it looked similar to a great white, megalodon was not a much bigger version of this famous modern shark. Its jaws were much wider, nearly 2m across, with over 250 large, serrated teeth, set in five rows inside the mouth.

Size estimates for megalodon have always been a problem, because we only have teeth and a tiny amount of its fossil skeleton preserved. The most recent research predicts most would have been around 10m long, some possibly 20m, which is the equivalent of three killer whales end to end. Weight is even harder to predict, but scientists believe adults weighed at least 60 tonnes, perhaps a lot more.

Megalodon could live in a range of marine environments, although younger animals seemed to prefer being close to the shoreline. It hunted a variety of prey: sizeable turtles, seals and whales, including huge sperm whales. It seems megalodon hunted by rushing up from below, attacking its prey's chest and biting into the ribcage to tear at the heart and lungs.

An adult megalodon needed over 98,000 calories every single day. Not only is this twenty times more than an adult great white shark requires, but it is the same amount of food an average ten-year-old human eats in six weeks.

TARSIER

(tar see-er)

ALIVE
45 MYA–NOW
ASIA
CARNIVORE

Our own branch of the animal family tree contains apes, such as chimps and gorillas; monkeys, such as baboons and macaques; and the famous lemurs from Madagascar, but the primate group also has a distant cousin that looks more like a gremlin.

The tarsier's head and body only measure about 15cm long, but its tail can add another 25cm. Its back legs, used for acrobatic jumping, can be twice the head and body length, giving us an idea of how powerful they must be.

It has huge eyes, with each as large, or even bigger, than its entire brain. To use its eyes to their full potential, the tarsier can turn its head 180 degrees, meaning that with one small turn, it can see all the way around itself, watching out for prey *and* predators at once.

This small nocturnal mammal lives in forests across parts of Asia, where there are types of vines called lianas, which it uses to climb up and down trees vertically. It moves by leaping from branch to branch and will jump on prey if it can. It eats a range of invertebrates, such as beetles, crabs, cockroaches and stick insects, as well as small lizards, bats, snakes and young birds.

The tarsier is the only member of our family group, the primates, that is completely carnivorous. Every other monkey, ape, lemur or loris is either a herbivore or, if it does eat other animals, is still an omnivore.

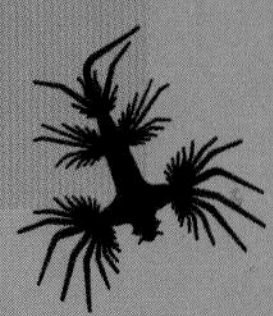

FLYING SNAKE

- ALIVE
- 25 MYA–NOW
- ASIA
- CARNIVORE

The flying snake might be better being called the 'gliding' snake, as it does not truly fly like a bat or bird. The five different species live high in trees, leaping into the air to escape predators.

Depending on the species, these brightly coloured snakes range in length from just under 1m to just over. The snake can climb a tree by using special ridged scales along its belly to push against rough bark and move up the tree with ease.

When flying, the snake's entire body makes a 'wing'. In cross-section, it is curved in a similar way to a Frisbee or flying disc. The snake's body flattens so much that it almost doubles in width, helping trap air beneath. The cross-section in these snakes and Frisbees causes air pressure beneath to increase, giving the snake (or Frisbee) lift, allowing it to glide better, and further. A flying snake can glide over 100m.

To glide, the flying snake hangs off the end of a branch and makes a J-shape, with its neck being the curve. Letting go of the branch, the snake quickly makes an S-shape, followed by a C-shape, which traps the air. By changing its body shape, the flying snake is able to turn and change direction while gliding.

The flying snake is mildly venomous, but its tiny fangs are right at the back of its mouth, meaning it is only dangerous to small prey, not to humans.

BASILOSAURUS

(bas-sillo sor-us)

EXTINCT
41-43 MYA
WIDESPREAD OCEANS
CARNIVORE

In contrast to its closest relatives, *Basilosaurus* had a very long and tapering body shape. Even its vertebrae (back bones) looked as if they'd been stretched. Whales evolved from four-legged land animals and *Basilosaurus* showed evidence of this. Fossils indicate it had hind limbs measuring 35cm long, with three little toes.

The teeth of the *Basilosaurus* did not all look the same, as they did different jobs, such as cutting and chewing. The teeth were full of complex lumps, bumps, grooves and channels.

Basilosaurus would have been at the apex of marine food chains. Evidence from fossil skulls and even stomach contents shows it ate sharks and other big fish, as well as smaller ancient whales, such as *Durodon*.

After all the huge, prehistoric marine reptiles went extinct 66 million years ago, there was space in the Earth's oceans for new giants. This ancient whale took the title of 'world's largest' for a few million years as the top predator in many marine environments.

Before giant modern whales evolved, *Basilosaurus* was possibly the largest animal on the planet for millions of years. It reached 17–20m long and weighed up to 15 tonnes, making it only 'medium sized' compared with today's whales.

When scientists predicted the power of *Basilosaurus's* bite, it was similar to that seen in alligators and crocodiles alive today. They estimated it was approximately 16,400N (Newtons). A Nile crocodile's is around 22,000N, your human bite (chewing) is 100–150N!

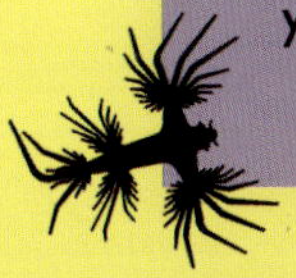

SPIDER-TAILED HORNED VIPER

ALIVE
10 MYA–NOW
ASIA
CARNIVORE

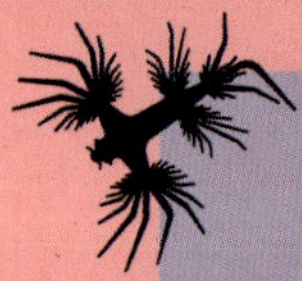

The spider-tailed horned viper's venom works especially well on birds. It can cause blood to clot, clumping together in a mere 13 seconds. When the blood clots inside the body like this, it can't flow and the bird dies quickly.

Imagine being a little bird, landing after a long migratory flight and hopping over to eat a spider, only to find out one of nature's biggest tricksters has set a deadly trap.

The spider-tailed horned viper can reach a length of 85cm or more, although most are around 30cm. Its scales appear rough, not smooth like those of many snakes, and are mottled in appearance, allowing the snake to blend perfectly with the sandy and rocky environment of its desert home. Like some other species of horned viper, it has scales that look like little horns above its eyes.

The most obvious thing about the spider-tailed horned viper is the feature on its tail that resembles a spider. The tip of the tail looks swollen like a bulb and is surrounded by slender scales that droop, looking just like legs.

The viper wiggles its tail back and forth along the ground looking like a tasty spider. It even holds its tail at a different angle, around 90 degrees, when trying to tempt prey. At that angle, the 'legs' dangle to look even more like a real spider. When the snake is within range, it can move at incredible speed and can strike its prey in 0.2 seconds.

BOBBIT WORM

♥ ALIVE
🕓 20 MYA–NOW
📍 ATLANTIC & INDO-PACIFIC OCEANS
🍴 OMNIVORE

Some unlucky people have found out the hard way that if you touch a bobbit worm, the venomous bristles running along its body can cause permanent numbness.

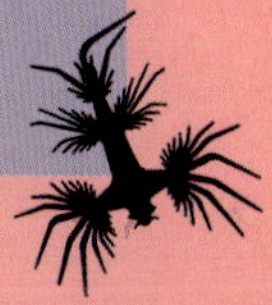

Worms are many things – wiggly, wobbly, even wibbly – but they're rarely weaponised. There is one giant worm however, known as the 'sand striker', that has a ferocious appetite, can move at lightning speed and has some rather impressive weapons.

The bobbit worm ranges from 10cm to over 3m long. Despite being able to grow to such an impressive length, its body, covered in venomous bristles, is incredibly thin. It might only be 25mm wide. Colours range from pale cream to bright purple and black. A rainbow-like sheen on the hard exoskeleton segments makes this worm appear to glitter when it catches the sunlight.

The worm lies buried beneath the sand, with only five antennae on its head visible. These are used to sense prey. When a fish brushes past them, the worm quickly catches its prey in a massive pair of scissor-like jaws, held open and ready to snap. Living in coral reefs, these worms also hunt among the corals, squeezing into tight nooks and crevices.

When it catches food, the bobbit worm turns its muscular, tooth-studded throat lining inside out, to 'swallow' its prey, dragging it into the safety of its burrow. As well as animal prey, it eats algae and dead or rotting material. Sometimes, the worm's massive jaws snap shut so quickly, it is said they can cut a fish in half.

GULPER EEL

ALIVE
~55 MYA–NOW
WORLDWIDE OCEANS
CARNIVORE

What's the biggest meal you've ever eaten? As big as your fist? As big as your head? What if you could eat something bigger than your entire body ... in just one gulp?

The gulper eel is long and thin, with no scales, like all eels. It reaches a maximum length of 80–100cm.

Many deep-sea fish have big eyes to see in the dark, but the gulper eel has tiny eyes, each measuring only 2.5mm across. Eyes this small can probably only sense light but not actually form images.

The gulper eel is named because of the way it gulps food into its massive mouth, which is larger than its entire body. The jaw attaches loosely to the head and can swing open to eat. There is no body behind where the jaw attaches, so nothing the gulper eel swallows can get 'stuck'. The jaw is so big it measures around a quarter of the total length of the eel itself.

Despite poor eyesight and not being a great swimmer, the gulper eel doesn't need to hunt prey. Food goes to it instead. On the tip of its tail is a lure that glows pink or red in the dark depths. When a fish swims over to investigate this interesting glowing light, it is met with a huge, gulping mouth instead.

The other name for the gulper eel is the 'pelican eel', after the bird famous for having a big mouth and an ability to swallow large prey.

DEMENTOR WASP

♥ **ALIVE**
🕓 **~70 MYA–NOW**
📍 **ASIA**
🍴 **CARNIVORE**

Imagine a hunter with the power to control its prey. One quick sting and it controls everything its prey does. It's the ultimate power for a predator. Even a small one.

This little wasp is around 10mm in length and is red and black, with slightly yellow wings. It has long, slender legs and a narrow 'waist', joining its abdomen to the rest of its body. It is known as an ant mimic, because it looks and moves a lot like an ant.

The dementor wasp has one of the most effective tactics of any predator in nature. It mainly hunts cockroaches and when it sees one, it stings it in the abdomen. This paralyses the cockroach for a time. Next, the wasp stings the cockroach directly in the head. This second sting blocks messages of 'fight or flight' in the brain, meaning the cockroach can't react.

The wasp then leads the cockroach by its antennae to the wasp's nest. There, it lays an egg on the belly of the cockroach. After hatching, the wasp larva burrows inside the still living cockroach and eats it from the inside out. The larva releases antibiotics to stop the cockroach getting infections and to keep it alive and fresh.

The dementor wasp gets its name from imaginary monsters from a well-known series of stories about young wizards. In the stories, 'Dementors' are feared for their ability to consume a person's soul, leaving their victims with a working body but without a personality.

TIKTAALIK

(tik taa-lik)

EXTINCT
375 MYA
N AMERICA
CARNIVORE

Life first evolved in water and for millions of years that's where our ancestors stayed. But we live on land so, at some point, something must have wriggled, crawled or slid from the shallows onto land. Tiktaalik was one of those early, land-living animals.

Measuring 1.25–2.75m, tiktaalik was a fish with features similar to four-legged land animals. It had scales and gills like a fish, but its bones were sturdy and strong, enabling it to walk around in the shallows and maybe on land for small distances.

It had a large, triangular head, looking more like the skull of a crocodile than of a fish, and its lower jaws could reach over 30cm in length. Its skull shows some evidence that tiktaalik may have had a pair of lungs, as well as gills, helping it live both on land and in water.

If you think about it, fish don't usually have a neck, do they? But tiktaalik did have a flexible section between its head and the rest of its body, which allowed it to be much better at snapping at and catching prey.

Tiktaalik lived at a time when pools, streams and lakes were low in oxygen, making it hard for life to survive in them. Walking between habitats and perhaps even breathing through lungs allowed this predator to survive where other fish could not.

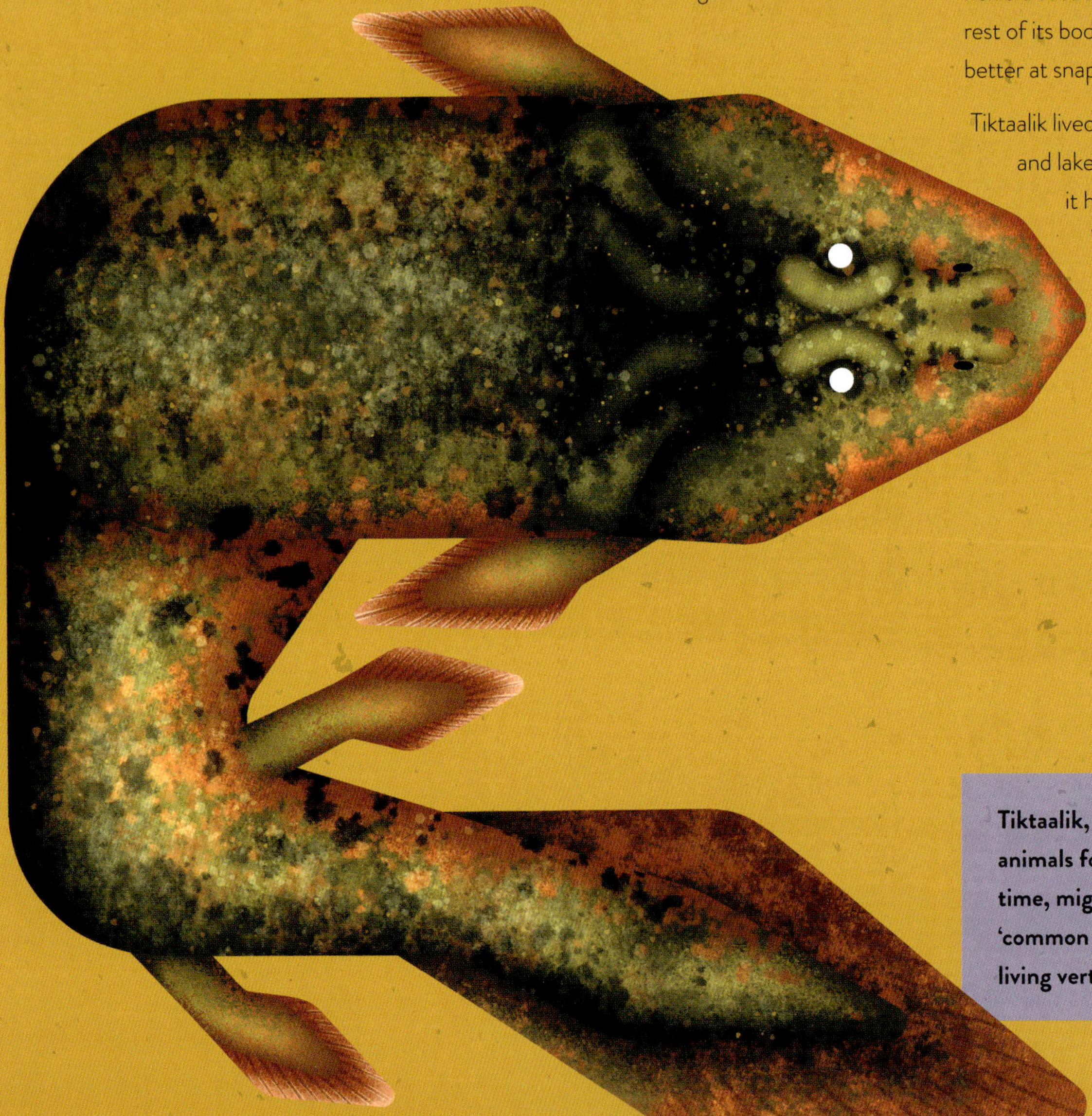

Tiktaalik, and several similar animals found around the same time, might be what we call a 'common ancestor' for all land-living vertebrate animals.

TAILLESS WHIP SCORPION

ALIVE
300 MYA–NOW
N AMERICA, AFRICA, ASIA
CARNIVORE

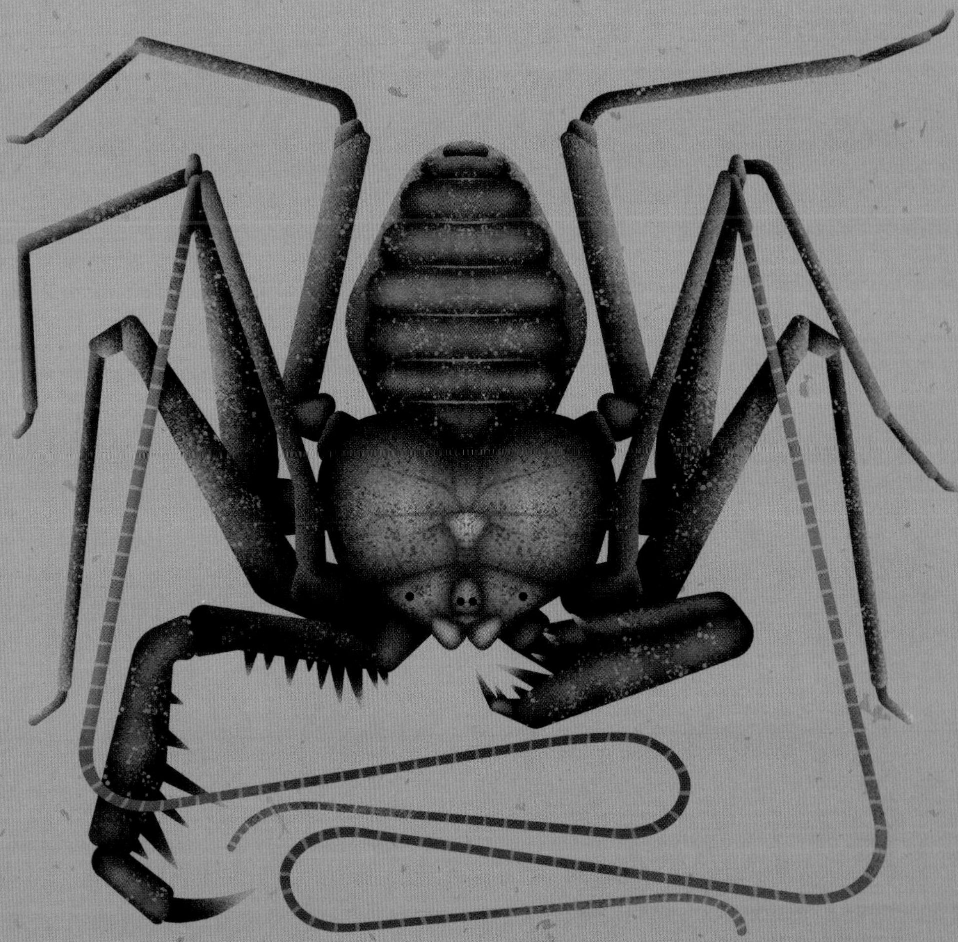

Many life forms look so strange, they could be the creation of artists or resemble aliens from a space film. Although the tailless whip scorpion might look imaginary, it is real.

Different species of whip scorpions are related to both spiders and scorpions. They are 25–85mm long and have eight pairs of legs, like their relatives, but only use three pairs for walking. The front pair are longer and thinner than the rest and used to sense the world around it.

Like a scorpion, a whip scorpion has a pair of pincers or claws at the very front, but unlike its cousin, it has an extra, large spine on these claws.

When threatened, it cannot defend itself with a venomous sting. Instead, it sprays a combination of two acids, which smell strongly and irritate the eyes of would-be predators.

The whip scorpion is mainly active at night, hunting millipedes, insects, slugs, worms and other scorpions. When it catches prey, it crushes it with special teeth-like structures on the insides of its legs.

A whip scorpion mother seals herself in a hole, where she will carry around 40 eggs underneath her body. For the next few months, she does not eat and barely moves. When the young hatch, they climb onto her back, where she can protect them.

When defending itself, the whip scorpion sprays acetic acid, which is the major ingredient in vinegar. Because the spray smells like vinegar, the other name for a whip scorpion is the 'vinegarroon'.

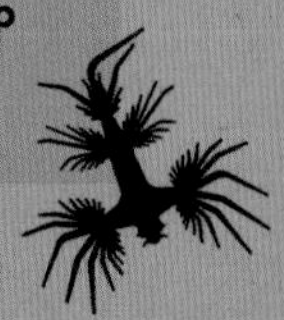

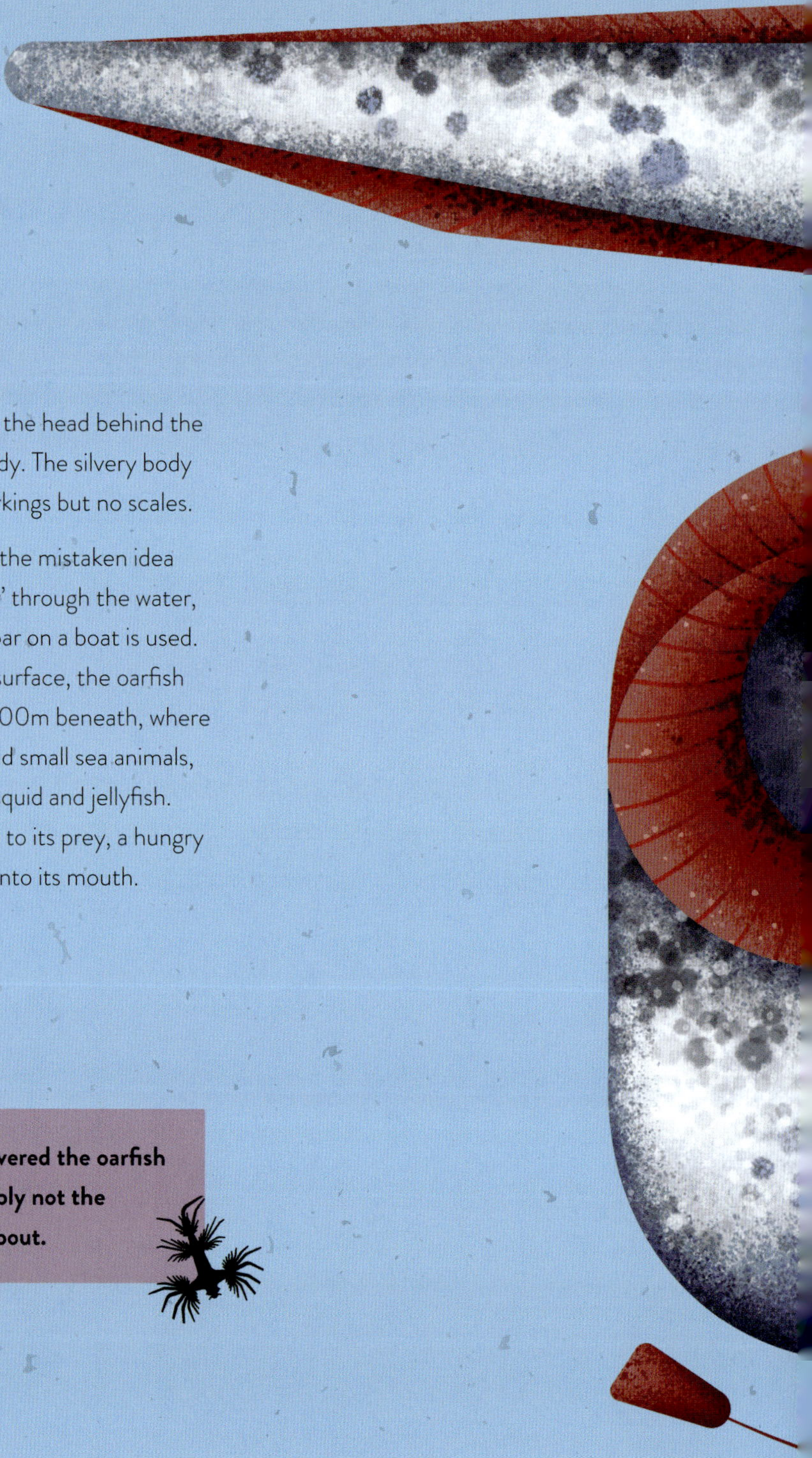

OARFISH

ALIVE
55 MYA–NOW
WIDESPREAD OCEANS
CARNIVORE

Although science has now shown it's not true, the oarfish was said to signal death for hundreds, if not thousands, of years. To see one washed ashore was a sure sign a terrible earthquake would soon follow.

The oarfish does not resemble any other sea animal imaginable, looking instead like a combination of fish and dragon, with added extra-terrestrial features. Measuring 8–11m long, but capable of reaching an almost unbelievable 17m, the oarfish is like a silvery ribbon, with a red-brown fin running the full length of the top of its body. It has large round eyes and a series of long red spines like a crown on its head. Slender red 'streamers' attached to the head behind the gills trail beneath its body. The silvery body has a series of dark markings but no scales.

The name comes from the mistaken idea that the fish would 'row' through the water, in the same way as an oar on a boat is used. Rarely found near the surface, the oarfish usually swims 250–1,000m beneath, where it hunts zooplankton and small sea animals, including shrimp, fish, squid and jellyfish. When it's close enough to its prey, a hungry oarfish sucks the food into its mouth.

Bizarrely, there is a single account from some scientists, who discovered the oarfish was able to zap them with electric shocks when touched. It's probably not the sort of thing many other scientists are lining up to find out more about.

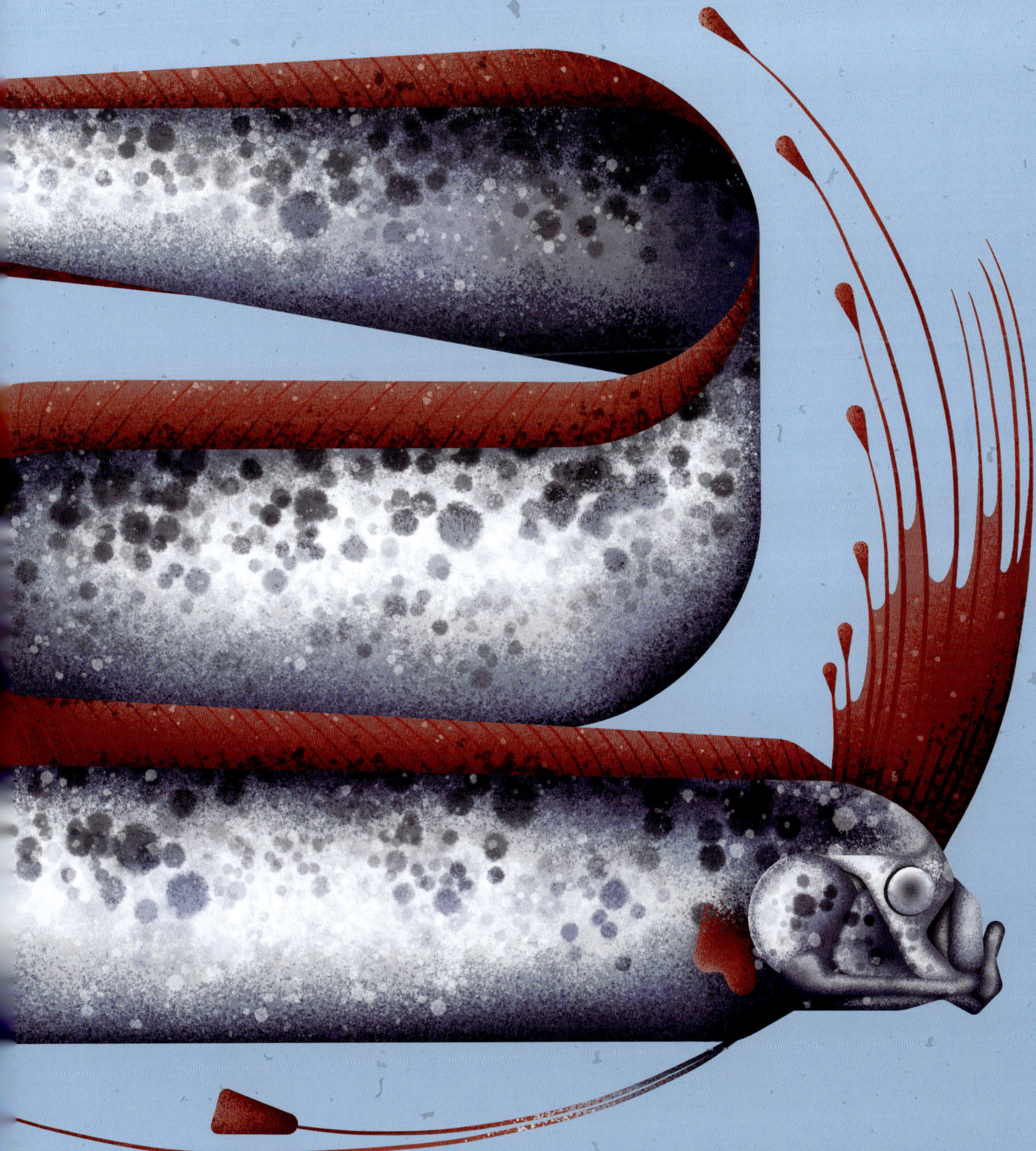

PATAGOTITAN

(pat-a-go tiy-tan)

- EXTINCT
- 101.6 MYA
- S AMERICA
- HERBIVORE

When a farmer went to look for some lost sheep he found the bones of what might be the largest dinosaur discovery ever.

Like other sauropods, *Patagotitan* had four legs that stood directly beneath a huge body. It had a long, muscular tail and a very long neck, ending in quite a small head.

Accurately estimating the size and weight of a dinosaur isn't always easy, because skeletons are often incomplete, and muscle, skin and organs are missing. From what we know, *Patagotitan* measured 31m long (the same as 31 large adult steps), and weighed around 57 tonnes. Compared to a more famous sauropod such as *Diplodocus*, *Patagotitan* would have been twice the height and over three times heavier.

Fossils show that the teeth were adapted for stripping leaves from branches. *Patagotitan* would have eaten tough plant material, like leaves from monkey-puzzle trees.

Patagotitan lived in forested areas along floodplains. These areas were full of conifer, or evergreen, trees, but fossils of ferns have also been found close by, giving us a good idea of what these giant herbivores ate. Although it would have been almost impossible to kill a healthy adult *Patagotitan*, predators such as *Tyrannotitan* lived in the same area at the same time and may have hunted young, sick or old animals.

The author of this book, Ben, was one of the very first people to go to Argentina and work with the team of palaeontologists, as they excavated the bones of *Patagotitan*.

GORGONOPS

EXTINCT
260-254 MYA
S AFRICA
CARNIVORE

When yawning or even when biting its prey, it's possible *Gorgonops* could open its mouth a staggering 90 degrees or so. If you're wondering, this is more than twice what you can manage.

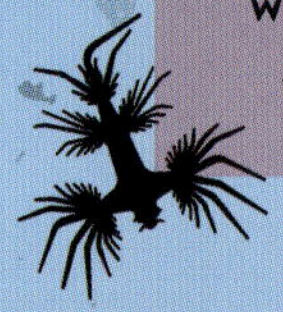

Named after ancient Greek monsters too terrible to look at, *Gorgonops* actually belonged to a group including our own (mammals) and our ancestors and close relatives.

There were many gorgonopsians, with *Gorgonops* perhaps being the most well-known of them. It was a medium-sized member of the group, ranging from 1.2–2m long from nose to tail. Its skull measured 22–35cm long and had some interesting features. When seen from above, the skull would have looked like a wide triangle.

Gorgonops had two very large canine teeth, measuring at least 12cm in length, which would have stuck out beneath the bottom of its lower jaw. The jaw helped protect these fragile teeth by being much thicker close to the canines and thinner towards the back of the jaw.

Gorgonops had a more upright body position than most animals alive at the time, meaning it walked and ran much faster and more efficiently than its competition and its prey. This allowed it to be a very successful predator within its environment.

ELEPHANT-NOSE FISH

♥ **ALIVE**
🕓 **5 MYA–NOW**
📍 **AFRICA**
🍴 **CARNIVORE**

Imagine if you and a group of friends could see out of each other's eyes in addition to your own. A similar type of instantaneous sharing of sensory intelligence has been found in a group-living, weakly electric fish from Africa.

The elephant-nose fish appears squashed from side to side, if you view it front on. It is dark purple or even black and has large eyes, triangular fins and a long, forked tail. It measures around 25cm in length.

It has a nose like an elephant's, although if you look closely, you'll see it's not the nose at all, but an extension of its mouth, with the lower 'lip' forming the elephant-like 'trunk'. This sensitive trunk is used for self-defence, communication, navigation and locating prey in the muddy water and riverbeds.

The fish lives in muddy, slow-moving rivers and pools, where there is cover from submerged branches. It is weakly electric, which means it can detect moving prey by creating incredibly brief electric pulses with an electric organ in its tail. Specialised groups of cells across its body, called electroreceptors, detect tiny ripples in the electric field made by objects, such as prey, branches or other fish that conduct or resist electricity.

Although you can't see the electric current made by the elephant-nose fish, it is possible to listen in. By dropping two little electrodes in a fish tank and hooking them up to a speaker, you can eavesdrop on their 'conversations' and find out how they're feeling.

When you think of a bird of prey, you might picture a huge eagle soaring in the sky, or a camouflaged owl silently swooping at midnight, but there is a member of this group that runs after its prey on its famously long legs and stomps on it.

It's easy to look at a secretary bird and think someone has stuck the head and body of an eagle onto the legs of a crane or a stork. Standing around 1.3m tall, about the same height as the average eight-year-old human, a secretary bird has legs nearly twice as long as other ground birds of the same body size. This allows it to have a unique hunting technique, using its legs and feet to strike and kill prey.

Secretary birds hunt in pairs or small family groups, moving through grassland habitats at roughly the same pace as an adult human walking. They are perhaps best known for being snake-killers, but snakes are only part of their diet, which includes mice, tortoises, chickens, insects and prey as large as adult hares and even young cheetahs.

A secretary bird stamps so quickly on its prey, the foot only remains in contact with the victim for 10–15 milliseconds, which is ten times faster than a human blinks.

SECRETARY BIRD

- ALIVE
- 29 MYA–NOW
- AFRICA
- CARNIVORE

LONGISQUAMA

(long-gee skwa-ma)

EXTINCT
235 MYA
ASIA
CARNIVORE

Meaning 'long scales', *Longisquama* is a small, extinct reptile, which lived about the time the first dinosaurs emerged on Earth. Although we only have one fossil skeleton, it tells us a lot about this mysterious animal.

Measuring only about 10cm, *Longisquama* had long legs, with large eyes and a fairly pointed head. Its most obvious feature was a number of long, thin structures that appear to have grown from its skin, running all the way between its head and base of its tail. We still don't really know how these plumes were held and if they stood up straight from the body or were held spread to the sides, for example.

With curved and pointed teeth, *Longisquama* ate insects and was able to bite through their hard shells. It hunted and lived in the undergrowth but also in trees, moving between branches.

The long, plumed scales running down *Longisquama's* back may have been used for gliding, or for clumsily slowing a fall or leap from the trees. It's more likely, though, that they helped the little reptile communicate or display, either to impress possible mates, or scare away competition.

Although some scientists have suggested *Longisquama* may have had the first feathers ever, and that we need to rethink how birds evolved, it now looks unlikely that this little reptile is closely linked to birds.

SUPERB BIRD OF PARADISE

ALIVE
~10 MYA-500,000 YA-NOW
AUSTRALASIA
OMNIVORE

Fighting for a mate can be dangerous! Having bright feathers or a loud call for dominance, or just being big and weighing lots takes up time and energy. Maybe it's sometimes better just to dance. Although this was the *only* type of superb bird of paradise, it is now properly known as the greater superb bird of paradise, or the greater lophorina (lo-phor ina).

A female bird of paradise is reddish-brown with dark bars on her underside. A male is midnight-black, with a blue-green covering down his chest and a metallic-looking green hood. He has a black cape running down his back.

To attract a mate, a male uses leaves to brush clear a patch of forest floor. Standing in the middle of his 'dance floor', he calls to attract a female. When she arrives, the male unfolds his black cape and his bright chest patch, which appears to form a big, dazzling shield around him. In the same way you may be able to click your fingers, the male then snaps his tail feathers against each other, while hopping about around the female in an elaborate dance.

When the male dances, his electric blue feathers appear to make a big smiley face, with two bright eyes and a big smile. He then dances by bouncing round the female rather excitedly.

BACTERIOPHAGE

(bak-teer ee-o fayj)

ALIVE
IT'S COMPLICATED
EVERYWHERE: LAND, WATER, AIR...
??

To be a life form means you have to be ... *alive*, right? The most numerous, commonly found organism on the planet has a DNA genetic code, hunts and feeds on prey and even behaves in certain ways, but it may not actually be alive. Amazingly, these alive/not-alive bacteriophage could hold the secret to battling our most terrible diseases.

Bacteriophages (or phages) are viruses that infect bacteria. They have many forms, some look like delicate dandelions, others like spaceships with boxy, 20-sided heads and robot-like, spindly legs. One of the most important features is the shape of its tail, allowing different types of phage to eat different types of bacteria.

There are, at the moment, around 8.2 billion (8,200,000,000) human beings on our planet, which seems like a lot, but when trying to work out how many bacteriophage there are, scientists predict around ten nonillion (that's 10,000,000,000,000,000, 000,000,000,000,000), meaning there are more bacteriophage than every other organism on Earth, including bacteria.

Bacteriophage means 'bacteria-eater', and they are bacterial parasites, eating the bacteria from the inside out. Like its bacterial prey, phage is found everywhere on the planet: in the deepest parts of the oceans, tropical forests, hot springs, sewerage, even on our skin.

Scientists are studying new ways to use phage to treat diseases, but first need to better understand these microscopic soldiers.

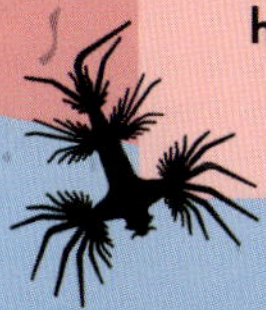

Take 4 or 5 droplets of water from a clean puddle or stream. There may be over two hundred million phage in the 4 or 5 droplets on your fingertip.

WHERE IN THE WORLD?

ASIA

ASIA
AUSTRALASIA
ANTARCTICA

WIDESPREAD & WORLDWIDE

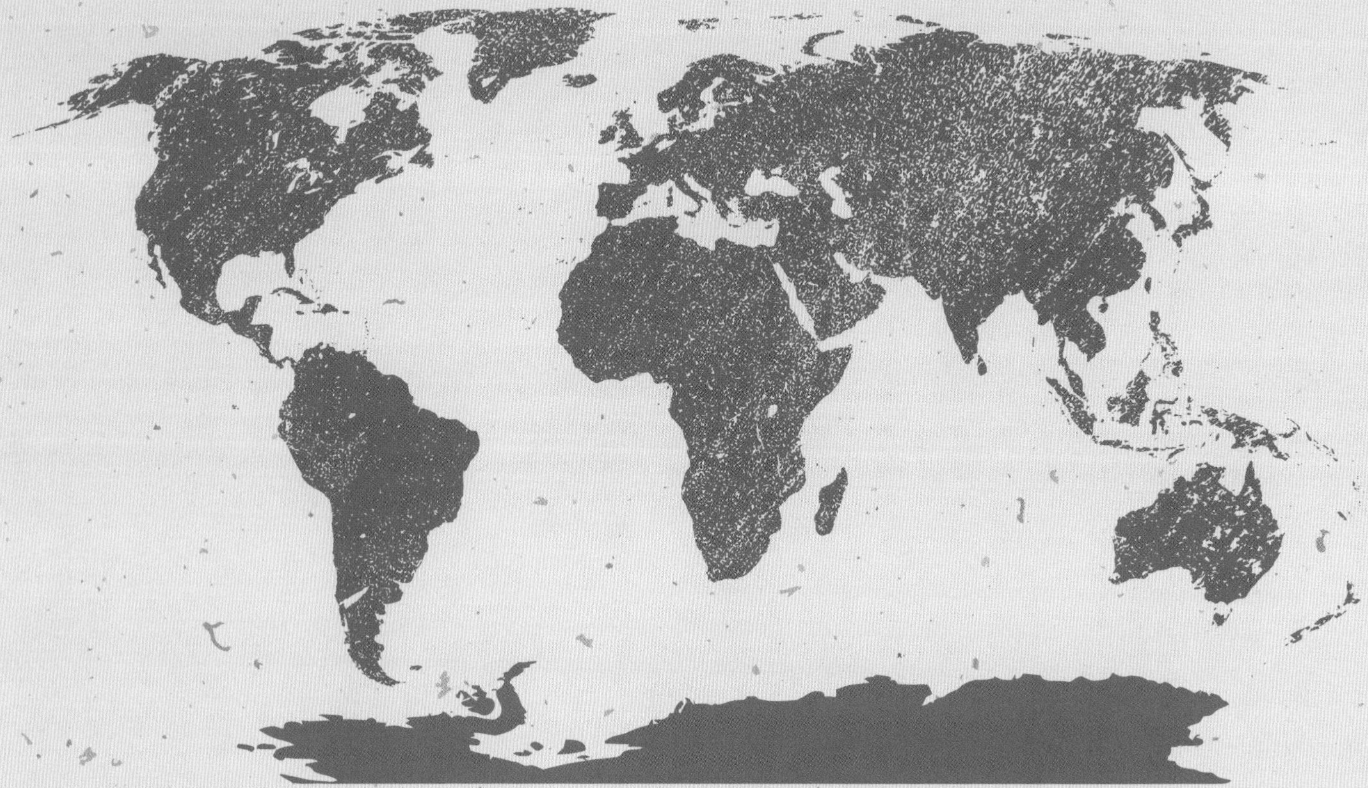

LAND

Antlion	♥	Worldwide, except Antarctica	92
Aphid	♥	Worldwide, except Antarctica	85
Bacteriophage	♥	Worldwide: land, water, air	143
Dung beetle	♥	Worldwide, except Antarctica	71
Dung cannon	♥	Worldwide, except Antarctica	46
Eurypterid	☠	Fossils from every continent, majority from North America & Europe	82
Firefly	♥	Worldwide, except Antarctica	96
Mosquito	♥	Worldwide, except Antarctica & Iceland	27
Silverfish	♥	Africa, North & South America, Australia, Europe, parts of the Pacific	121
Tardigrade	♥	Worldwide, including Antarctica & oceans	117
Tarantula wasp	♥	Worldwide: India, Southeast Asia, Africa, Australia, the Americas	86
Velvet worm	♥	Worldwide tropical habitats & temperate zones of the southern hemisphere. Central & South America, Caribbean islands, equatorial West Africa, southern Africa, north-eastern India, Thailand, Indonesia, Malaysia, New Guinea, Australia & New Zealand	95

OCEANS & SEAS

EUROPE

Cordyceps	♥	North America, Europe, East & Southeast Asia: China, Japan, Nepal, Vietnam, Bhutan, Korea, Thailand	22
Deinotherium	☠	East Africa, southern Europe, South & Central Asia	44
Dimetrodon	☠	North America, Europe: Germany	14
European eel	♥	Europe, North Africa & Sargasso Sea	97
Fiddler crab	♥	West Africa, western Atlantic, eastern Pacific, Indo-Pacific, Portugal	80
Midwife toad	♥	Europe & northwestern Africa	120
Saiga antelope	♥	Kazakhstan & Russia	34

AFRICA

Animal		Location	Page
Aye-aye	♥	Madagascar	47
Basilosaurus	☠	Egypt, Western Sahara, Morocco, Jordan, Tunisia, Pakistan, southeastern USA, Peru	127
Deinotherium	☠	East Africa, southern Europe, South & Central Asia	44
Elephant-nose fish	♥	West & Central Africa	139
European eel	♥	Europe, North Africa & Sargasso Sea	97
Fiddler crab	♥	West Africa, western Atlantic, eastern Pacific, Indo-Pacific, Portugal	80
Gaboon viper	♥	Sub-Saharan Africa	116
Giraffe beetle	♥	Madagascar	42
Gorgonops	☠	South Africa	138
Midwife toad	♥	Europe & northwestern Africa	120
Naked mole-rat	♥	Eastern Africa	30
Sarcosuchus	☠	Africa: Niger, Morocco, Tunisia, South America: northeastern Brazil	65
Secretary bird	♥	Africa	140
Shoebill	♥	Central tropical Africa, from southern Sudan & South Sudan to eastern Congo, Rwanda, Uganda, Western Tanzania, Northern Zambia	66
Tailless whip scorpion	♥	Africa: Senegal, the Gambia, Guinea-Bissau, North America: Arizona, New Mexico	133

AUSTRALASIA

CENTRAL AND SOUTH AMERICA

Amazonia giant centipede	♥	Northern South America: Aruba, Brazil, Curaçao, Colombia, Venezuela (including Margarita Island), Trinidad	62
Axolotl	♥	Mexico	94
Basilosaurus	☠	Egypt, Western Sahara, Morocco, Jordan, Tunisia, Pakistan, southeastern USA, Peru	127
Bullet ant	♥	Central & South America: Honduras, El Salvador, Nicaragua, Costa Rica, Panama, Venezuela, Colombia, Ecuador, Peru, Bolivia, Brazil	78
Glyptodon	☠	South America	53
Hoatzin	♥	South America: Amazon & Orinoco basins	64
Manchineel tree	♥	Caribbean, Florida, Bahamas, Mexico, Central America, northern South America	84
Milkweed assassin bug	♥	Southern North America, Central America, South America (except Chile)	103
Patagotitan	☠	Argentina	136
Potoo	♥	Central & South America	48
Sarcosuchus	☠	Africa: Niger, Morocco, Tunisia, South America: northeastern Brazil	65
Smilodon	☠	North & South America	16
Terror bird	☠	South America & North America (Texas)	32
Thylacosmilus	☠	South America: Argentina	114
Titanoboa	☠	South America: Colombia	23
Vampire finch	♥	Galápagos Islands	57